Also by Thomas J. C. Martyn

Aviation Adventures:
The True Story of the World War 1
Royal Flying Corps Pilot
Who Founded Newsweek

Inside the Founding of
Newsweek

How a Hot-Tempered, One-Legged R.A.F. Pilot Launched an American Media Giant

By

Thomas J. C. Martyn

with a foreword and afterword
by his granddaughter, Anne Martyn Alexander

Inside the Founding of Newsweek

Copyright © 2015 by Anne Alexander

ISBN 978-0-9852380-2-5

Cover design by Yavni Bar-Yam

www.InsideTheFoundingOfNewsweek.com

Dedicated by Anne Martyn Alexander
to her father, Howell C. Martyn,
as well as intrepid journalists
and visionary entrepreneurs
everywhere

Table of Contents

Foreword

When I was 16, I visited my grandfather, Thomas J. C. Martyn, at his home in southern Brazil for six weeks. On my return, I carried the manuscript of this memoir, which he wanted my father and me to get published. That was the first time I really became aware that my grandfather was the founder of *Newsweek*.

A huge formal oil portrait of him hung on the dining room wall in the house where I grew up; the actual man was rarely seen. In the painting, he was dressed in his military uniform, and he stared down on us with a steady gaze, an odd reminder of the man missing in my father's life. Despite his constant presence above our dinner table, he was rarely spoken about and his remarkable accomplishment of founding *Newsweek* was never discussed.

My grandfather—known affectionately as Gpa (jee-pa), for that is how he signed his letters—was an Oxford educated British citizen who became a pilot with the British Royal Flying Corps (later called the Royal Air Force) at age 18, as World War I began. He contributed several innovations to the military effort and lost a leg in a plane crash. As kids, my siblings and I thought his wooden leg to be quite exotic: on the few times we got a glimpse of it, we stared with fascination.

In 1923 he was invited to join the editorial board of *Time* magazine as its first foreign editor, and helped Henry Luce and Briton Hadden launch the publication. With his second wife Helen (my grandmother), he was drawn into the glittering party scene of the time, joining the orbit of business magnates, judges, blues singers, and other artists of the day including F. Scott Fitzgerald, his wife Zelda, and Thornton Wilder.

After leaving *Time* magazine, my grandfather worked for the *New York Times*. According to his memoir, this is when the idea of someday starting his own weekly news magazine began to form. As history proves, he correctly assessed that there was room for more than one such publication in the market-place.

In 1932, he assembled a group of wealthy businessmen, including Paul Mellon and Nelson Rockefeller, and, as chair-man of the board and the first business manager, launched *Newsweek*. The first issue was published February 17, 1933, a scant few months before President Roosevelt declared a three-day "bank holiday", one of the lowest points of the Great Depression. One American worker in four was unem-ployed, businesses were failing at the rate of 230 a day, and newspapers were called "Hoover blankets"—valued as much for their warmth as for their information. Tougher times in which to start an enterprise like *Newsweek* could not be imag-ined.

Despite the shaky financial times, my grandfather travelled around the country, seeking advertisers and testing the waters to see how his new magazine was being received. He met with businessmen and politicians, including Henry Ford, who offered to take him on a personal tour of the River Rouge plant; the president of the Goodyear Tire & Rubber Company; Harvey Firestone of Firestone Tire & Rubber Company; the president of the Packard Motor Company; and President Franklin D. Roosevelt—my grandfather declared himself "impressed, despite myself, with his impelling personality and captivated by his seductive charm of manner."

In *Inside the Founding of Newsweek,* my grandfather lays out how he undertook the herculean task of launching a news magazine to challenge *Time.* In his often searing assessments of the people involved in this huge undertaking, he does not spare himself. He refers to his "excesses of temperament" and the fact that he was "at times too outspoken, caustic, and bad tempered," and confesses: "One of my many handicaps is having Celtic blood in my veins. When Celts are up they are very, very up, and when they are down, God help them."

All the same, my grandfather seemed to have the respect of most of his team, being described by the head of the newspaper guild as "tough but just." He writes "I thought that ... the finest tribute ever paid me." He pursued his vision with the fierceness and near round-the-clock hard work most every entrepreneur knows. He was optimistic, decisive, and totally dedicated. He tried to hire the best people he could, and stayed focused on data and analysis, not just gut feeling.

Despite all that he brought to the venture, my grandfather had a series of fallings-out with the board of directors. Eventually a merger with Vincent Astor's Today magazine was negotiated and he was removed from the board, paid off with "severance pay" of $10,000, and forced to sign a general release that deprived him of any future financial stake in the magazine he had created.

I have worked in business most of my career. I, too, have worked the insane hours, put everything at stake, hired, fired, sweated, hit walls, failed, re-emerged, and survived. Re-reading my grandfather's memoir from the vantage point of middle age and 12 years as a business coach and consultant, the years and distance between us dissolved. I found many threads linking his entrepreneurial story and mine, such as his story about Starling Childs' business planning tip, which he applied too late to his *Newsweek* endeavor. Childs, one of *Newsweek*'s original investors, had made his fortune building utility plants. He told my grandfather that once he figured out what he thought a project or launch was going to cost and the amount of time it would take, he doubled the monetary figure and quadrupled the amount of time to get a more realistic projection. Childs' calculations accurately reflected what it would take *Newsweek* to become successful. Before I became familiar with my grandfather's story, I myself told my clients to double the amount of money and time they thought they needed to launch their business—and with rare exception, it has proven to be true.

Other key entrepreneurial lessons in this memoir include the need for decisiveness even when information is insufficient (which it always is), the danger of giving jobs to investors, and the importance of written agreements.

Not long after his shocking dismissal from the *Newsweek* board, my grandfather went to South America on a new business venture, leaving behind his wife and two young children (my father and my aunt). He wanted them to join him, but according to my great aunt, "Argentina looked too uncertain to Helen [my grandmother] with two children." Then World War II broke out and, with German submarines off coastal waters, it was not considered safe to travel. My grandmother went to live with her father, Howell Cheney, part of the Cheney silk magnates of Manchester, Connecticut. When her father remarried she moved into an apartment and got a job. So from the age of six my father was raised by an essentially single mother. A dutiful son, he kept in touch with his father through letters, seeing him occasionally when he returned to the State for visits, but I do not believe that he ever forgave him. His sister, my Aunt Laura, never did.

So great was the betrayal of being driven from the company my grandfather founded, the dream his entire career heretofore had been building up to, it seems to me that he literally left the continent. His attorney believed that the general release my grandfather was asked to sign "would be worth the paper it was written on," which is to say it could not possibly be binding. Yet the attorney also held that there was no effective way for my grandfather to secure himself stock or a percentage of the corporation, because Vincent Astor and his partner Averell Harriman would "find means and ways of eliminating my interest or reducing it to a negligible amount." My grandfather writes that he was the largest stockholder in *Newsweek* and that the general release was basically extorted from him. Yet in all of these dealings he felt compelled by a higher duty than self-interest: "As the father of *Newsweek*, my first duty was to my magazine. I had to keep it alive at whatever cost to me." And so he was forced to sign away any interest in what went on to become one of the greatest news publications in United States history.

Ultimately, what he desired more than a financial stake in the magazine was recognition in the form of his name on the masthead. In this account, he writes that "my bitterness and disappointment receded into the past and were eventually forgotten." That may well have been true, but on his gravestone in the municipal cemetery of the small, rural town in southern Brazil where he lived in his final years, he chose to have the words "Founder of *Newsweek*" inscribed. That's how proud he was of his accomplishment and that's how significant it was in his life.

Practically strangers except for letters, my grandfather and I only spent time together in person three times. He came to visit my family in 1961 and we went on a family beach vacation, but being only two years old at the time, I don't remember that trip. He also visited in 1968. The last time I saw him in person was in 1975, when my younger sister and I went to stay with him in southern Brazil for six weeks.

On my return home, I carried in my suitcase the manuscript that forms the basis for this book. Subsequent letters from my grandfather made it clear that he wanted my father and me to try to get it published. In 1977, he wrote to me saying that he intended to draft another important document on *Newsweek*, and that he would send it to me when he finished. He died two years later, his important document unsent.

Always the good son, my father kept his emotions to himself and never prevented me from writing to my grandfather. But my father had essentially been abandoned by him at the age of six, so he rarely spoke about my grandfather and, according to my mother, was very bitter about him. So my father was unlikely to do anything to advance my grandfather's interests by getting his memoir published. As for me, at the time I was sixteen, preparing to go to Switzerland for a year on a student exchange program and then to college, and I did not give the manuscript much thought. It ended up on a shelf in my father's closet. For 34 years it sat there, along with my father's unresolved anger. My siblings and I rediscovered the manuscript after my father's death; with the benefit of my life experience I could see its inherent significance, which had escaped me before.

At that time my grandfather's oil portrait was moved to my brother's house. Now as an adult I studied it afresh and realized that my nose was strikingly similar to his and very unlike the noses of my father, mother, and siblings.

It struck me that I also inherited his entrepreneurial "gene," which no one else in my family has, or, to be honest, wishes they had, as well as his fiery temperament. As an eight-year-old, I bought candy from the local grocery store and sold it at a profit to my mother and sister. I ran a foot massage business, rubbing my father's feet for one cent a minute (or two cents a minute for "super first class" which included corn huskers lotion). I founded Anne's Advertising Agency, which provided signage for my customers' needs, primarily my father, who ordered signs about closing the chimney flue and other household directives.

I was also a blooming writer. My father gave me a used manual Royal typewriter from the insurance company where he worked, and as a pre-teen I produced four novels and assorted poetry, as well as *The Weekly Newspage*, which consisted of neighborhood, local and regional news, book reviews, quotes, jokes, recipes, sports, and biographies of historical figures such as Gandhi, Robert Frost, Roald Amundsen, and Benjamin Franklin. Going through old letters from my grandfather many years later, I realized that he was an official subscriber of *The Weekly Newspage* (one dollar for 20 issues), and I discovered an astounding and poignant letter regarding my journalistic effort, which clearly drew on his own experience in publishing.

May 13, 1970

Dear Annie:

Another *The Weekly Newspage* has come and has been, so to speak, devoured. It is getting better, and steady improvement is a big leaf in your crown of laurels. I know of nothing quite like it, and have never known anything like it. It is original, informative, and entertaining. Keep it that way.

Starting a publication, any well-intentioned publication, is an act of friendship. You make friends with a lot of people, many of whom you will never know. And they will not only make friends (sometimes critical friends) with you, but they will begin to rely on you as well as support you. The fundamental difference between you and them is that all of your public will get to know you.

So, whether you like it or not, your reputation becomes involved, if not at stake.

You are with every new issue contributing to a chapter in the annals of American Journalism. You are entitled to be proud of yourself. Have you ever thought of it that way?

Much love,
     Gpa

As a child, I had no idea that in my own small way I was following in his footsteps and what that might have meant to him. In my grandfather's letters to me over the years, he showed himself to be a delightful correspondent and a loving and supportive grandfather, despite being thousands of miles away. As his granddaughter, I didn't have the history with him that my father did, and I was able to see my grandfather in a more balanced way. I wish we had been able to have a relationship from which I might have learned more about his amazing accomplishments, not only with *Newsweek*, but with his experience as *Time* magazine's first foreign editor, and before that, his wartime experience as a pilot. Of course, I also wish my grandfather had had a stronger attorney at the time of his ouster from *Newsweek*, because perhaps he could have reached a much better outcome.

Nonetheless, until my grandfather's memoir resurfaced when my father passed away, I rarely even thought to tell friends that my grandfather founded *Newsweek*. It was as if what he achieved—and lost—was a kind of open family secret. Since I carry in my genes both his entrepreneurial and his journalistic traits, I felt compelled to share the story he drafted. I hope that his side of the story, in all its fascinating detail, will help redeem his accomplishment and fill out the story of a great magazine's history.

In addition to taking whatever lessons you may draw from these pages, I hope you enjoy the ride.

Anne Martyn Alexander

Prologue

This prologue has been reconstructed from Thomas J.C. Martyn's letters, papers, and other documents from the family archives.

# # #

There are few enterprises more speculative and demanding than publishing. For that reason only the rich, those well able to afford a loss, can enter into the Kingdom of the Fourth Estate by the front door. There are no reliable tests that can be made to predict the success or failure of a publishing venture, much less the amount of money it will take to make it profitable. Anyone who presumes to forecast the outcome of such a venture is not much better than a charlatan.

Of all the events in my life that I did not and could not predict, the most bitter occurred one spring morning in 1937 when I entered the *Newsweek* offices for the last time. I remember it as clearly if it had happened yesterday and I expect I always will. I passed through those doors in a state of tumult knowing that the staff, every one of whom I had hired, would be planning a farewell for me. A truer farewell had taken place some weeks earlier, when Marvin Pierce, then provisional publisher of *Newsweek*, presented me with a general release that, with my signature, would sever me from the newsmagazine I had founded.

Never, when I held the first issue of *Newsweek* four years earlier, would I have anticipated such an outcome. My vision for this newsmagazine was far-reaching, my desire and expectation being to expand the market beyond the one and only such publication then available, *Time* magazine. In my mind's eye I saw a second newsmagazine providing readers with news that spanned the world, but told with sobriety, accuracy, and depth. This publication would be less rigid and departmentalized than *Time*, responding instead to the important news at hand. The photographs would convey the stories of the day as effectively as the reporting, and the cover of the first issue of *Newsweek* demonstrates that very principle. Seven pictures illustrate the days of the week in news: Nazi troops, a new aviation distance record set, Hitler and his cabinet, Roosevelt and his advisors, the U.S. Navy at battle practice, Stalin.

Would I compete with *Time*? Most certainly. Would the contest benefit both parties? Undoubtedly. The realities of newspaper competition demonstrated my case. Almost any big city in the United States accommodated several newspapers, so it did not require much imagination to see two profitable newsmagazines co-existing in the entire United States.

Rivalry would expand the market for newsmagazines, I reasoned, and that has proven to be the case. I believed there was a field unplowed, and our team set to sharpening its plow.

It was a poor time for us to start plowing. We could not have picked a worse one, for as our first issues of *Newsweek* reached the newsstands in February 1933 the nation's financial institutions were collapsing. A month later, a wave of bank closures swept through almost every state in the nation. A quarter of the civilian work force was unemployed that year; March was the worst month for joblessness in the history of the United States, with fifteen and a half million people out of work. Our new President, Franklin D. Roosevelt, proclaimed that "the only thing we have to fear, is fear itself". That was most certainly true in business at the time: fear stopped the hand of investors, at the very time we needed their confidence the most.

Even so, *Newsweek* was backed by a number of multimillionaires whose combined fortunes must have stretched into billions of dollars, even in those days. Providing I could demonstrate within a reasonable length of time that *Newsweek* was a certain money maker, I thought myself invincible. It never occurred to me that in the face of certain future profits my backers would withdraw their support from me. But that is exactly what happened.

Any successful venture will breed its challengers. I faced increasing opposition from various parties who wished to occupy my seat as publisher, or at the least oust me from it.

Though each time I saw them off, confidence is a fragile thing, and gradually that of my board was shaken. There came a time when they acted without me, meeting behind closed doors and excluding me from decisions regarding the "brain-child" I had sired. All of this came to a head with the proposed merger of *Newsweek* with *Today* magazine, Vincent Astor's "adventure in political journalism". Within a year, I was asked to release my interest in *Newsweek* for absolutely nothing in return.

Chapter One

Time Magazine

The day was bright, sunny, and cold when I arrived in New York aboard the *Olympic* early in February 1923. A fresh fall of snow gave the streets a dazzling coat of pure white, which soon turned to a grimy black from the then little understood pollution of the air. But on that day I thought New York was truly beautiful, and I read into its beauty a hopeful and happy omen.

The streets fairly exploded with energy, all of its five million inhabitants seeming to spill on to them at once, by foot, trolley, taxi or motor car. America was the world's wealthiest nation and New York was at the heart of its commerce. In the streets around Times Square, men paraded in their tuxes, silk-lined topcoats, and patent leather shoes, while elegant women in evening gowns mingled with young flappers in short skirts and bobbed hair. Dance marathons competed with jazz musicians of the likes of Louis Armstrong for the public's attention. Nightclubs and theaters brimmed with reveling patrons most nights of the week. Cinemas drew patrons in with exciting new films: *The Hunchback of Notre Dame* and *The Ten Commandments* were released that year.

Time magazine met me at the dock in the person of E.E. (Ted) Paramoor, a friend of Briton Hadden, and as soon as the Customs and Immigration formalities were over he escorted me to the Yale Club, which was to be my residence for the next month. Hadden, a Yale man, had arranged quarters for me there and it was a hospitable home for my first weeks in New York. Before its opening some eight years earlier, diligent Yale Club members had scrutinized other clubs to determine the most comfortable chairs for the lounges, while a committee set itself to ensuring that the wooden tables were sufficiently sturdy to resist all traces of alcohol that may be spilled on them. The club's patrons ensured this research was not wasted as we ensconced ourselves and drank copiously.

Once my luggage was safely stowed in my room, Ted took me to 9 East 40th Street where *Time*'s office was located, a single room that spilled over with writers and researchers. The heating was turned off at weekends, and in late February it was so cold that the staff were huddled over electric heaters and typing in their overcoats. There I met for the first time Briton Hadden and Henry Robinson Luce. Both received me with marked kindness.

The next day I started work for the first time in my life as a journalist on the first-to-be-printed dummy of *Time*. On that day I met my future colleague Manfred Gottfried, with whom

I shared office space and later on a modest apartment on Lexington Avenue until my family arrived from Europe. During that first week I met the whole *Time* staff, all of whom appeared to regard me, as an Englishman in their midst, with considerable curiosity. Many of them went out of their way to make me feel at home. I particularly recall Roy E. Larsen in this respect, who later on put me up at the Harvard Club. The circulation manager for *Time*, Roy was an energetic and determined man, whom a colleague described as a "grim but smiling terrier".

Briton Hadden was assiduous in introducing me to his friends and members of his family. Through him I met John Stuart Martin, then a senior at Princeton and soon to become one of the most important members of *Time*'s staff. When he became engaged to Mimi Bushnell I was invited to a dinner given in their honor and became duly impressed with the size of the Bushnells. Mimi herself was a towering woman with dazzling blue eyes and curly red hair. Father, mother, brother, and the bride-to-be were each in a six-foot class, or thereabouts. I met Steve Benét, the poet, and his wife Rosemary. A somewhat frail man in round glasses, Steve was a good friend of John Carter and that is how I got in touch with him. Both he and Rosemary were very kind to me. I also worked alongside his brother William Rose Benét, twelve years his senior and a writer too, who was married to that high-strung poetess Edna St Vincent Millay.

Through Ted Paramoor I met, dined, and reveled with F. Scott Fitzgerald and his wife, generally in a nightclub. His wife Zelda frightened the life out of me with her uninhibited talk, to put it mildly. Incessant partygoers, they were both prone to making fools of themselves with their theatrical displays and exhibitionism. It was not unknown for them to leap into the fountain at the Plaza Hotel, or for Zelda to remove her clothes and dance naked. Other people who flitted across my early panorama of New York were Philip Barry, Thornton Wilder, Thayer Hobson and his good wife Priscilla, and many others that escape remembrance, all of them incipient literary lights.

Through Briton Hadden I came to know William T. and Maude Hincks, who almost adopted me, so often was I a guest at their house in Fair Haven near Bridgeport. Hincks, a lawyer and founder of Hincks Bros. & Company investment bankers, was a director of *Time* and father of Hadden's Yale classmate John M. Hincks.

No foreigner ever had a warmer welcome to the United States and my social life soon became extremely pleasant and interesting. At first, when we had not much money and there was the matter of Prohibition to be got around, *Time*'s staff would gather in a speakeasy; Briton had his favorite on Third Avenue, where a secret knock gained us admittance and we drank bootleg liquor from teacups.   Later with Briton I enjoyed many a lunch at the Hotel Algonquin, always a lively place to dine, favored as it was by New York's writers, actors, and intellectuals. Most days you could see a famous face or

two: *New Yorker* founder Harold Ross, perhaps, or Dorothy
Parker, sharing gossip and witty barbs with her set.

After the first dummy of *Time* came off the press Briton
took me downtown to the editorial offices of the *New York
World*, a gold-domed building on Park Row. We traveled by
subway, the fastest method to traverse the city even then, and
a pleasant enough journey in the carriages with their wicker
seats and ceiling fans. There I was introduced to Herbert
Bayard Swope, its brilliant, forceful and stentorian editor and
Hadden's former boss. A tall man with a booming voice and
carrot-red hair, Swope was a bold editor who had broken stories on the sinking of the *Titanic*, corruption in the police force,
and the Ku Klux Klan. He was even better known as a party-
giver, and it is said that his neighbor F. Scott Fitzgerald mod-
eled scenes in *The Great Gatsby* on the almost never-ending
party that took place at Swope's house in Great Neck.

Our visit was for the purpose of seeking Swope's valued
opinion of the dummy issue. Swope promised to read it and a
date was fixed for our return to hear the great man's pro-
nouncement. When we next were ushered into the presence
of this super-energetic man (I have always referred to him as
"one mighty Swope" after one of J. Ryder Haddard's characters who killed I don't know how many of what with "one
mighty swipe"), he was evidently not in a good humor. The
copy of *Time* lay before him on his desk and as he turned over
the pages, accompanied by thunderous vocal declamation, I

could see that it had been heavily marked. After a severe criticism of the National Affairs section, which was apparently all that he had read and in which he could see no good, he advised Hadden to give it up and come back and work for the *World*. In a brief lull before the session ended I plucked up enough courage to ask him what he thought of the Foreign News section. He replied laconically that it was "all right". I did not think he had read it.

Hadden was furious and when we left the *New York World* building he walked so fast to the subway entrance that I almost lost him in the crowd, a not small quandary for a stranger in New York. The next day Hadden was himself again, more determined than ever, fortunately for all concerned.

Swope was one of Hadden's idols and it is gratifying to report that neither of them lost respect for the other as a result of this incident. Swope became an original subscriber to *Time* and remained for Hadden a paragon of an editor whom he copied in many ways, consciously or unconsciously.

# # #

Briton Hadden was to become one of my best and closest friends. We were to live together after *Time*'s return from its short sojourn in Cleveland. How that came about was typical of Brit, as I shall call him hereafter. One day he called me at the *New York Times*, where I was then working, and ordered me, no nonsense about it, as was his manner, to meet him for lunch at his favorite Hotel Algonquin on a matter of great importance.

As soon as we were seated at the table Brit told me, without any preliminary sparring, that he was about to borrow $25,000 from his grandfather, President of the Brooklyn Savings Bank, to buy himself an apartment. He did not want to live alone any longer and had chosen the only two people with whom he would like to live: William J. Carr and me. A friend of Brit's from his Yale days, Carr was a young lawyer on the rise, though until then I had never heard of him, much less seen him.

I could hardly believe my ears. I am by nature far too credulous for my own good, but this demonstration of friendship I could neither credit nor accept. I pointed out that he must have many and older friends than I with whom he would prefer to live. He would not listen. His mind was made up. I told him I was immensely flattered and said I would think it over and asked him to do likewise. He said he did not have to think it over. He wanted my yes or no there and then. To put the screws on me a bit tighter, he added that if I would not or could not agree, he would not buy the apartment. As I was foot-loose and fancy free, I gave in subject to a look-see at Carr.

Characteristically Brit had thought it all out beforehand: I was to meet Carr the next day at the Algonquin. He would not be on hand himself because he wanted Carr and me to get to know each other without any pressure from him. If we liked each other and thought we could get along together, that would be enough and it would be a deal. I was not so sanguine. It seemed to me highly unlikely that two men who had never met could get to know each other well enough over a single meal to want to live together. Moreover Brit himself was an unknown quantity in this respect. Anyway, the meeting with Carr took place the next day as scheduled and, happily, we took an instant liking one for the other, a typical Irish-American and a more or less typical English journalist. It was almost unbelievable. Brit was immensely proud and pleased with himself and cemented the deal by inviting us both to Southampton for 10 days. As a result of that lunch I gained another and much beloved friend—a friendship that lasted until Willie was killed in North Africa during World War II.

Brit's is still a difficult character to analyze. He had what I should call a kaleidoscopic personality; it all depended through which facet you viewed him. When he was on his best behavior, he was affable and charming. At his worst, he was a boor. He had enormous reserves of energy and iron determination. His friendships were more real than apparent. Months could go by without a sign from him. In fact, he was sometimes critical of his friends, apparently on the theory that if they were good enough to be friends with they were good enough to criticize. Let anyone else censure them and the Champion was up in arms in their defense. This was particularly true of his relationship with Luce in the early days of *Time*.

One of his most outstanding traits was a mischievous sense of humor, a dangerous weapon in the mind of an editor. He had two paramount passions: baseball and words. As far as I could determine, he had little interest in women. He liked them and they liked him, but something in his make-up, probably his shyness, made him feel awkward in their presence.

Once he invited Judge Robert L. Luce, a relative of Henry Luce, and Libby Holman, a popular blues singer of that time, to dinner. Judge Luce, a distinguished-looking lawyer, very conservative and a bit on the serious side, was pitted against the husky-voiced Libby, who had no looks but a super-keen wit. Libby was famous for many things, among them her strapless dresses and her romantic liaisons. Brit hugely enjoyed putting two such disparate people together and we all enjoyed the repartee that ensued. The Judge was in seventh heaven. So was Brit. And Libby was at the top of her form. The party was a great success, and the gaiety maintained its momentum throughout a game of Hearts, one of Brit's major vices, which he played badly, forever "shooting the moon" without a rocket, so to speak.

Brit took me several times to the brand-new Yankee Stadium to see a baseball game. Set on the former site of a lumberyard in the west Bronx, the stadium was twice the size of any other ball park and able to seat 58,000 spectators. Brit had his rituals there, and would wave down the hotdog man to buy eight, because Brit was a "four-hotdog man". I was not a bit interested in the game. To me, it was the old-fashioned English game of rounders, only played with a hard ball and a round bat, plus some fancy rules. But I more than enjoyed Brit. In fact, I was enchanted with his enthusiasm and knowledge of the game and the individual players in it. He loved to make forecasts of what this and that player would do at the bat, and he was frequently right.

As an editor, Brit was an enigma. With a relatively limited range of knowledge on the one hand, he was a veritable genius with words and syntax on the other. He had a gleeful passion for Homeric double adjectives, solid short Anglo-Saxon words, and inverted sentences such as that made famous by *The New Yorker*: "Where all this will end only knows God." *Famous* became *famed* (one letter shorter), *gum-chewer* described the *hoi polloi* but *bandy-legged* was preferred to *bow-legged* (two letters longer). And so on. When the news was served up in a desecration of the English language, particularly when it applied to personalities in the news, many were offended, many were amused, many applauded.

Brit was a difficult man to work for, but so great was his enthusiasm for what he was doing that the onus of writing for him disappeared. He never wrote a line himself but sent stories back to the writer, or newspaper clippings with cryptic notations that served as instructions. When he was satisfied with a story, he literally chortled with mirth, as he did when he encountered a word new to him. Most of these were contributed by the writers themselves and adopted by Brit. One exception was Brit's choice of *tycoon* for *magnate* (one letter shorter). There was some discussion about its adoption and I offered the word *shogun* (same length) in its stead, but *tycoon* won the day. Brit never spared himself or anybody else in these daily verbal acrobatics. Until I got used to what I thought of as Brit's editorial eccentricities, stories would come back to me two or three times before they were entirely acceptable to Brit. Gottfried (Gott), who was a much better writer than I, fared little better. What was required was to join in the fun and fury and out-Brit Brit in word formation and "syntimetax". Thus Gott and I and many other writers contributed many words that were incorporated into *Time*'s lexicon.

The work was hard and the hours were long. Our team would write, cut, paste and pin the galleys through the night, then see the issue off the press just before dawn. The working week was most often seven days long, and it never eased up even when we got used to Brit's idiosyncrasies. I was hired to write foreign news, but so great was my own enthusiasm that it never crossed my mind to protest at the extra work that was piled upon me. As I got more and more proficient in the Brit-*Time* style, I soon found myself rewriting stories from contributors that did not please our exacting editor. Many of the early contributors were fired for non-conformance and until they were replaced the load fell on Gott and me. At one time we were writing or re-writing close to two-thirds of the magazine.

We even found time to try our hand at writing some circulation promotion literature, which was even more certainly not in the contract.

Thus was born a new type of journalism. The essential task was to pare stale news to its intrinsic facts, garnish it with a background appropriate to the subject, and serve it to the reader in an easily assimilated form. The formula succeeded miraculously, despite its prosaic texture, and that was due uniquely to the drive and genius of Briton Hadden. *Time* style was often fresh in the true and vulgar meaning of that word.

Brit's conversation was also *Time*-style, punctuated by a good deal of growling and gnashing of teeth. These odd manifestations were not a sign of anger or frustration. On the contrary they were evidence of deep satisfaction. Behind his mannerisms and below his sometimes-abrupt demeanor was a very shy man, which few people suspected. And to some extent he was naive. This ingenuousness combined with his social timidity often made his meanings obscure. One early morning after the magazine had been "put to bed", Brit approached one of *Time*'s researchers and suggested that they go for a carriage ride around Central Park. This more than somewhat disconcerted her. Was the big boss of *Time* trying to make a pass? And what might happen if she refused? And she *was* about to refuse, on the excuse of weariness, when something in Brit's expression, something in his eyes, prevented her from doing so. She decided that in any case she was a big enough girl to take care of herself. So she went. During the whole time, she told me later, he talked of himself, his work, his hopes, and his worries. Just a lonely man needing someone to talk to. No pass.

When Willie Carr, Brit, and I were living together part of the contract was that we would take on Brit's maid Olive. We did so. Olive was a huge, cheerful woman who looked after us extremely well until we found out at the end of the first 60 days (less ten days we spent together in Southampton) that she had been looking after herself extremely well also. Brit presented each of us with a bill for close to $1,000. Both Carr and I thought it was very reasonable and offered to pay our share of it then and there—very reasonable until Brit informed us that the princely sum of almost $1,000 was our individual share! We discovered that the good Olive had been taking home and lavishly distributing to her numerous family whole hams and joints of meat and it must have been a carload of groceries. The butcher's and the grocer's accounts were astronomical.

We held a meeting and decided that both Olive and Brit must go—Olive forever and Brit as self-appointed treasurer. It was typical of Brit to insist on bringing Olive with him. She had served him well in his former abode, where he did no housekeeping. It was likewise typical of him to leave the unpleasant job of getting rid of Olive to Willie Carr. He thus showed his loyalty to Olive and demonstrated his keen sense of justice in consenting to her dismissal and his own demission. All done with good grace and much growling and tooth snapping.

After Olive's departure we had a Filipino houseboy who was almost the personification of Wodehouse's Jeeves insofar as service went. His name was Ro, and what a man he was! He kept the eight-room apartment spotless and performed the work of three valets. He was an excellent cook to an unusual extent for he could produce a four or five course dinner for three to a dozen people at the drop of a hat. And the hat dropped frequently. Brit and Willie Carr, who did most of the entertaining at 25 East End Avenue, were in the habit of forgetting to tell Ro how many guests they would have for dinner, not that Ro did not ask each of us at breakfast every morning. Willie would usually telephone Ro after consulting his memorandum pad in plenty of time for him to make the necessary arrangements. But Brit seemingly never knew who or if he was going to invite, and if he did rarely told Ro about it, which amounted to the same thing. He would storm into the apartment between six and seven at night calling, "Ro, there will be four more to dinner tonight," or simply walk in around 8 o'clock with his guests. Ro was never heard to complain.

It was not uncommon to have up to a dozen guests, which meant that a dinner that lacked nothing in quality or quantity would be served anywhere between 10 o'clock and midnight, depending on the number of guests. Meantime there would be canapés to make and drinks to serve, an impossible task for one man. But within minutes, Ro would have three or four adjutants on hand to help with the cooking and serving. He never charged for this extra help and somehow or other never ran short of anything, food or drinks. I once asked him how he did it. He explained to me that none of his people knew how to play fan-tan. The inference was that he played well enough that they all owed him money and paid him back in service. The real reason, I suspect, was that they all received handsome tips from our guests and us. Ro took the greatest care of us and our interests and when I remarried later on he asked me to take him with me.

Brit's tremendous energy, his acute sense of justice, and his tough determination were never better illustrated for me than by the incident of the torn coat. The episode was in itself a bit puerile to my mind, but not to Brit's who felt himself outraged. He had been in Hoboken one night and had taken a taxi to or from somewhere or other. As he got out of the taxi (read *exploded* for *got*) one of his coat pockets got caught in the door handle and tore. An angry Brit blamed the taxi driver. One can only imagine what the taxi driver told Brit as he drove off leaving our incensed hero fuming on the sidewalk, but Brit's sense of injury was real, not imagined. He was honestly convinced, judging from the vehemence of his invective, that the taxi driver was responsible, and he was determined to get back the money it cost him to have his coat repaired. To that end he got himself a Hoboken telephone directory from which he selected an address as far as possible from the taxi company's dispatching office. He then set his alarm clock for a pre-dawn hour and telephoned the company to send a taxi urgently to that address. He continued this routine until he thought he had got his money's worth. Then he quit. It is not known if the taxi company ever caught on. One may argue that the game was not worth the candle, but one cannot gainsay Brit's extraordinary persistence.

# # #

Brit once told me that a man's a fool not to borrow all the money he needed while he was young. He had all his life to pay it back. But he'd better be right, he warned. Brit had just done that and he had been right. His ambition was to make a million dollars by the time he was thirty. He may well have done so. By the time he was 31 he had certainly done so—though he never knew it, because he died in February 1929. His shares in Time Inc. were appraised at just over $1,200,000, which he left to his mother, Mrs. Elizabeth Busch Pool. Of these she sold slightly more than a million dollars of shares, which her son, Crowell Hadden III (half-brother of Brit) invested for her in shares of the Gillette company, a specialty of his brokerage company. The oncoming Depression practically wiped out the value of this investment, however, and it was fortunate for Mrs. Pool that she had kept 500 *Time* shares, for sentimental reasons, which increased over the years enough to make her a multimillionairess before she died.

As a little boy, Briton Hadden had the first glimmerings of a newsmagazine when his already fertile mind gave birth to *The Daily Glonk*. His experience with *The Glonk* carried over to the *Hotchkiss Record*, which he edited for a time, and on to *The Yale News*, of which he was twice chairman of the board. It is recorded that when Hadden asked Herbert Bayard Swope for a job on the *World* he stated that his reason for wanting the job was to "get experience to help him start a paper of his own." And it is related that he was fond of talking to his colleagues on the *World* about the paper he intended to publish on his own.

Fate then took a hand in the promotion of Brit's newsmagazine in the person of the writer Walter Millis, a classmate of Hadden's at Yale. Walter's boss, Frank Munsey, was anxious to attract some new blood to his publishing empire at $40 per week. He asked Millis if he knew of anybody. He did. He remembered his classmates Hadden and Luce and wrote them two identical letters offering them jobs on the *Baltimore News*. Brit wrote on the bottom of his letter "If we are ever going to start that paper, this looks like our chance", and sent it off to Luce in Chicago.

This communication is the first concrete evidence that Brit had already interested Luce in his ideas for that "paper". The "paper" was still undefined, though it was very much alive in Brit's mind. There does not appear to be any other evidence, except talk, some of it schoolboy talk, and reports of talk. Luce can be pardoned for not taking Hadden's visionary ideas too seriously at the beginning and for having accepted the offer of a job with the International Harvester company. That he was prevented from taking it was surely one of the luckiest things that ever happened to Luce, for it enabled him to hitch his wagon to Brit's star. The known facts and his mother's oft-repeated assertions establish that Brit was the leader, the dynamo, that led to the founding of *Time*. Luce was the follower, a valuable and useful one, and second in command. To an unusual extent they complemented each other.

During my two and a half years with *Time*, Brit was the editor for most of them despite the fact that an agreement between the two rivals—for such they were, ardent and intense—had established that each would alternate as editor every six months. The breakdown of that accord was more of Brit's work than Luce's. The editorship was Brit's domain by right, for at least as long as he could persuade Luce to stay on the business side. No doubt about it: Luce outshone Brit on the business where, as Prince of Pennypinchers, he performed miracles, which Brit openly admitted. Although Brit was no fool with money, in my opinion he was incapable of doing what Luce had done for *Time* in its formative years.

There was always the faint suggestion that Brit kept Luce in his place: that is, where he wanted him, and he was not above using Luce for any unpleasant task that cropped up. Brit's seniority in the enterprise was doubtless fortified by the fact that the cost of launching *Time* had been met wholly or mostly by Brit from money borrowed from his family. Wholly, according to his mother, who probably lent some of it to him.

Harry Luce was the complete opposite of Briton Hadden. In fact two more dissimilar men would be difficult to imagine. Whereas Brit was shy but friendly, generous, and hospitable, Luce was cold, aloof, parsimonious. I never met any of Luce's family. He never invited me to lunch or dinner or bought me a drink. I thought the poor guy just didn't have the money for any display of generosity. Both he and Brit received $30 a week in those days. Luce had to live on that slender stipend. Brit did not, because he lived for free at home.

Luce lacked Brit's flair when he was in the editorial chair. His attitude to the news was quite different, much more scholarly, less imaginative, often dull. Nevertheless he was a good workmanlike editor, and he really worked at it, which made him much easier to work for than for Brit. But he was no fun at all. I remember writing a piece on religion for him that ended with a flourish on the words *God the Father.* The typesetter, by design or in error, had changed the final *r* of *Father* to a *d*, making the word *Fathed.* Nobody caught the error, and thus it was printed. A storm of protest and cancellations followed, signal evidence that *Time* was a well-read magazine. Luce was most upset when he called my attention to the lapse. I am afraid the pagan in me made me more amused than outraged.

Under Luce's editorship I found the magazine uneven and inclined to stodginess. I think that was partly because Luce was not always in favor of *Time*'s style as architectured by Brit. The result was that the sections written by the regular staff remained loyal to Brit's style, whereas the sections contributed, which more or less always had to be doctored, bore the impress of Luce. Brit evidently felt something of the kind himself, because he returned every issue edited by Luce to him heavily marked with his gigantic pencil, in the same way that Swope had scored the dummy issue.

Harry Luce was born in China, the son of a well-regarded missionary. His father, Henry Winters Luce, was a classmate at Yale of Frank Dexter Cheney, an uncle of my second wife, and of Cyrus McCormick of International Harvester fame. According to Frank Cheney, it was Mrs. Cyrus McCormick who financed part of Harry Luce's education in the United States and generously supported the father's good works in China. Because of this, many people were shocked when, years later, Luce permitted the publication in *Fortune* of an article critical of the International Harvester Company and the McCormick family in terms thought to be in poor taste considering how much Harry owed the family.

That Harry Luce was an overtly ambitious man is an inescapable conclusion. Once soon after my arrival in New York we were walking together on lower Park Avenue when a beautiful glossy Cadillac passed us, glittering in the sunshine. "One day," said Harry to me, "I am going to buy one of those cars." Before he was through with this vale of life he could have bought fleets of them, but at the time his observation marked him as an ambitious man. There is nothing against ambition, on the contrary a great deal to be said for it in any young aspiring human being, provided acceptable norms of behavior are not abused. To Harry Luce the ends were more important than the means. That is the Harry Luce I knew. He well may have mellowed as affluence and a beautiful and intelligent wife overwhelmed him.

In June of 1926 Briton Hadden, then in Cleveland, was petrified to read in a local newspaper that his Alma Mater, Yale University, had bestowed an honorary degree on his partner, Harry Luce. Recovering from the initial shock and unable to believe his eyes, he set about confirming Luce's departure from Cleveland. Numbed by what appeared and what actually *was* Luce's perfidy, Hadden set off for New York himself in order not to be on hand when Luce returned from the East.

My future father-in-law, Howell Cheney, was a member of the Yale Corporation that made the award. Years later I asked him why Yale had given a degree to Luce and not to Hadden, who was the heart and soul of *Time* and who was more responsible than Luce for the outstanding contribution to American journalism, the reason for the award. His answer was that there was only one degree available. I then asked him why the award had not then been given to Hadden in preference to Luce. He replied that it was because Luce had a better academic record than Hadden. I asked him what that had to do with subsequent achievement, but received no answer. Obviously the Yale Corporation had made not the slightest effort to find out who was the most responsible for the success of *Time* up to that point.

While every friend of Briton whom I then and afterward knew was of the opinion that a great injustice had been done and that the degree should have been bestowed on Hadden, this carried little weight with Brit. The degree in itself meant little to him. What stabbed him to the heart was that Luce could accept the award without a single word to him. Considering what Luce owed to Hadden and what they both meant to each other, Luce's sly exit from Cleveland can only be construed as an intentional slap in the face, an act particularly unworthy of a friend and partner. That is how Brit looked at it.

Soon after Brit got to New York he telephoned me to have a command lunch at the Algonquin. There he poured out his version of the incident. I never again saw him so upset. He left me in no doubt that any friendship that may have existed between the two protagonists had come to an end. I asked why they could not find some way of parting company. He said he couldn't, and that he would work with the devil if he could make money that way. And so it was. The sense of injury did not pass and there was no "deep mutual respect" on Hadden's side. Brit never forgave Luce. His mother was much more virulent and she neither forgot nor forgave what he always referred to as Harry's "treachery."

# # #

While Harry Luce forgot what he owed to Briton Hadden (he even tried to terminate the Briton Hadden Memorial at Yale, of which I was a trustee, without reference to me), they both forgot many people who had helped them to make *Time* the success it was to become. When I first became aware that *Time* was preparing to write its history, I wrote a series of nine letters to Luce exhorting him not to forget the men and women who had helped him mightily on his way to the top. One of them was Briton Hadden. I suggested that he acknowledge his debt to Hadden by putting his name on the masthead of *Time* as a co-founder. This was only done after Luce's death.

Another was John Franklin Carter. John was, indeed, not forgotten in the history, later published as *Time Inc: The Intimate History of a Publishing Enterprise.* He was mentioned just twice: once in connection with his recommendation of me as the first Foreign Editor of *Time* and again when Luce fired him at Hadden's request because he could not write. This accusation shows Brit as irresponsible as Luce in their relations with some third parties. But it was not quite what Brit meant. The import was that he could not write the way Brit wanted him to. Many writers had the same trouble with Brit, and Carter was not the first to be fired because he could not write—for him. It is not difficult to imagine that John Carter would consider Brit a literary oaf and his style of writing sheer murder of the English language. Yet, the irresponsibility remains. Carter was at that time an experienced foreign correspondent and subsequently became the author of a brilliant newspaper column under the pen name of Jay Franklin as well as the author of several political books. Aside from this, both Brit and Harry were heavily in debt to John.

What the published history of *Time* did not relate, possibly because the editors were ignorant of the facts, is told in part in a letter from John to me in September of 1965:

In the winter of 1921–1922, during the Washington Naval Conference, I was approached by Harry Luce and Brit Hadden, who were then working on a Baltimore newspaper, to join in making plans for Time *(it was provisionally called* Facts *in those days). They, I, and Walter Millis, who was working on Frank Munsey's Baltimore paper, met at* Baltimore News *several times in Baltimore and Washington, and later we all went up to New York and got seriously to work. I understood I was to have a stock interest in the paper and spent about two months working with them (Millis had dropped out of the picture) until May when I accepted a commission from the Williamstown Institute of Politics to go to Europe and round up lecturers for future sessions. I left my* Time *affairs with my brother Henry, now deceased, but when the time came for incorporation I was frozen out.*

Granted that this letter is not accurate as to some of the detail, it does point out one interesting fact: that they got seriously to work only when they got to New York. Up until that time there had been a great deal of general discussion about the idea of a newsmagazine that would keep people informed, but very little of the magazine itself. The actual planning started when they got to New York and continued for several months. Who paid the expenses of this pre-publication period? According to Carter and confirmed by Brit's mother, it was Brit himself who financed the venture. Carter paid this own living expenses and only once received money from Brit for traveling expenses from New York to Boston and return when he was sent with the prospectus to get an opinion of it from Dr. Charles W. Eliot, the preeminent academic and former president of Harvard. The opinion? "Horrible."

During the two months that Carter worked for the magazine, he made some valuable contributions. He worked with Brit and Harry on the prospectus, whole phrases of which are redolent of John's literary style. Presumably it was because of his work on the prospectus that John was sent with it to interview Dr. Eliot, an important mission. Carter also contributed two departments to *Time*: Point With Pride and View With Alarm, intended to take the place of a newspaper editorial. In the hands of a mischievous-minded Briton Hadden, these sections became pure dynamite and had to be dropped. Carter also coined the word *newsmagazine*.

After *Time* had begun publication, Brit asked me if I thought I could persuade John Carter to come back to the USA to be *Time*'s National Affairs editor. I answered that I knew John was planning to return to the States just as soon as his contract with the *London Chronicle* was up, which I thought was imminent. A cable was sent off in my name offering him the job at $60 a week. To this honorarium was added the princely sum of 5 percent of the eventual net profits. Even tied to the net profits of *Time* as distinct from Time Inc, this percentage would have amounted to many millions of dollars over the years to come. There seems little reason to doubt that the 5 percent was designed to cover not only future work but to reward him for his gratuitous pre-publication collaboration. In other words it was to take the place of the promised stock interest. The offer of the job and the percentage was obviously based on unlimited confidence in John and appeared to be an honorable discharge of Hadden's and Luce's obligation to him.

How can we then explain his subsequent ignominious dismissal? John Carter was as much of an entrepreneur as Hadden and Luce and his status as such was recognized by the offer of a stock interest. Not only that but what he gave to *Time* was applauded by Harry Luce. Surely he deserved the title of the third co-founder. Despite all this he got nothing, not even an honorable mention.

Doubtless involved was a clash of personalities and temperament. John had had a brilliant academic career at Yale and was sometimes inclined to be a bit short with his more illiterate brethren. He could thus irritate Brit without meaning to or even without knowing that he did so. This could explain John's difficulty with Hadden. I had no such trouble. Without previous experience and without a talent for writing, I found it relatively easy to conform, or rather join in, the development of *Time*'s style of writing, particularly as I had had some practice in the art of précis writing.

Years later, triggered by my experience with *Newsweek*, long after his claim had any legal validity, Carter wrote to Luce inviting him to waive the statute of limitations. When that failed he asked him to settle on a sporting basis, declaring that he had all the necessary documents to prove his claim. There was no answer. John then suggested a settlement on a moral basis, leaving the amount to him. Luce was sufficiently impressed to send a man to John and together they discussed the claim. Nothing ever came of it. Luce had evidently intended to enjoy his immunity behind the statute of limitations.

My own experience was parallel. I had come 3,000 miles across the ocean, which had not cost *Time* a cent, at *Time*'s invitation to be its first foreign news editor first at $60 a week then at $100, plus a generous 500 shares of stock in the enterprise under a buy-back agreement in case I resigned or was fired. Since I was evidently giving satisfaction to my employers I felt thoroughly safe and settled in my adopted country. I had bought a house on Long Island and had moved in with my wife and two small daughters.

Suddenly, like a clap of thunder out of a clear sky, came the news that the whole staff had been fired, but that our jobs would be waiting for us in Cleveland, Ohio. This was exclusively Luce's idea. Hadden fought against it until Luce convinced him that *Time* would save $20,000 by going there, which it did not. Through Brit's intervention it was finally agreed to pay my railroad fare to Cleveland, but not those of my wife and children, so I was left in an impossible position. Much as I wanted to go, the expense involved alone precluded it.

I did not resign. *Time* just moved away from me. No attempt was made to help me find a new job, bearing in mind that I had no other contacts in New York save *Time*. Not a single introduction to anyone. No dismissal pay or the equivalent. I was simply left on the street.

At almost the twelfth hour of the last day set for redemption in our contract, Luce appeared with the money to redeem the 500 shares of stock. Had I been experienced in such matters, or had I known of a good lawyer, I might have successfully refused to hand over the stock. I had not resigned, and I was not technically fired because my job was waiting for me if I wanted it. It had been merely transplanted to Cleveland. Later on in a friendly discussion with Brit, I said that I thought in all fairness I should have 50 shares returned to me. Brit seemed to agree, but nothing came of it because, soon after, he died.

One wonders idly what might have happened to the Carter–Martyn claims had Brit lived. The only certainty is that *Time* would have acquired a ball team.

Thus my brief connection with *Time*, pleasant and instructive as it had been, came to an ugly end.

Chapter Two

The Beginning

Most people want to know: When did you first think of *Newsweek*? What made you think of it? Did you intend it to be a magazine like Time? What was your policy? Why did you call it *Newsweek*? And so on. To be meticulously precise I did not begin to think of my journalistic venture as *Newsweek* per se until the latter part of 1932, when I coined the name exactly as it is today, that is without a hyphen. And as Newsweek I shall refer to it throughout this memoir.

At the time I came up with the name, there was considerable argument about it. We had fixed on the dummy name of Tribune for the purposes of the prospectus and some of my colleagues were in favor of that name over *Newsweek*. The majority of them thought that *Newsweek* as a single word would not be understood by the public. Since I insisted on the name, I had to give way on the hyphen and thus it became registered as *News-Week*.

It was always my intention to consolidate it into a single word whenever we thought the public - our public – would approve. Malcolm Muir, who became my administrative successor under Vincent Astor and Averell Harriman, apologized to me for having dropped the hyphen, but I reassured him by saying that I had intended eventually to drop it myself.

Abstractly I thought about the idea of *Newsweek* many years before while I was working for Time Inc. as its first foreign editor. One of the operations that fascinated me was the way Roy Larson, then the magazine's circulation manager, secured subscriptions. Although my interest at the time was purely academic, I went into the cycle of procedures with infinite pains, studying each detail, and finished up with a great respect for Roy as well as a comprehensive appreciation of his work. And I suppose that subconsciously my interest in Time's circulation methods must have been the starting point of my subsequent plans for a second newsmagazine. This was certainly putting the cart before the horse because concretely I had not thought about such a venture.

A chance remark of Briton Hadden's somewhat later on may have galvanized my latent thinking about it. Brit said to me in substance: "A man's a fool not to borrow every cent he can lay his hands on while he is young. He has his whole life to pay it back. But he'd better be right." Hadden, the genius of Time, and his partner Luce, had done precisely that, raising an initial $87,000 with which to start the publication of Time.

It was not until Time moved back to New York from its temporary sojourn in Cleveland while I was on the staff of The New York Times that I first began to think definitely about another newsmagazine. I talked to Briton Hadden about it, particularly stressing the inevitability of competition. He took some convincing, but he finally agreed with me, as he did with my contention that Time should be proud if one of the first Timers actually did the founding of it. Luce on the other hand, whose vision was in inverse ration to his ambition, subsequently took a very different attitude, accusing me of trying to put Time out of business. Looking backward over more than a third of a century, such an accusation appears ridiculous and was probably meant to ridicule me, but it would have been entirely in character for Luce to have been uncased over the advent of *Newsweek*. Since it was not in my own interest even to have thought of putting Time out of business, which I certainly did not do, I took the charge as being an attempt to belittle me, in which it did not succeed.

While I never had any idea in mind, in my talks with Briton Hadden, that Time would take a direct or indirect interest in my projected plan for a second newsmagazine - I suppose it is better to call it a dream in those days – I undoubtedly was hoping for some sort of blessing and perhaps even passive cooperation. I got just the opposite. I have often wondered what would have happened had Briton Hadden lived. That is of course just another dream without any significance whatever.

It may be said that the success of Time, to which I had modestly contributed my iota, the abundance of news material, the availability of excellent news services, the infinity of possible interpretations of news and attitudes to it, as well as the very large number of profitably competing newspapers, were elements that subconsciously and progressively influenced my decision to start *Newsweek*.

A contributing factor and perhaps a decisive one occurred while I was on The New York Times. I had suggested to Lester Marvell that the Sunday Times print a summary of the past week's news in the form of a separate supplement. The idea of a synopsis took hold and is a feature of the Sunday Times to this day. For some reason or other Marvell did not adopt the idea of a New York Times newsmagazine. It was then that I said to myself that someone is going to do it one day.

As to the title of the proposed newsmagazine my first choice was the single word NEWS. It was short, expressive and apposite, much more so than Time. My collaborators and counselors were by no means unanimous. The hebdomadal implication was of course absent. The debate was cut short by the entrance of a legal doubt: the name was protested in the context of the Daily News. I argued that it was doubtless protected by a hundred other newspapers using the word news in their mastheads. Cautious counsel agreed, but pointed out that our capital would be for the publication of a newsmagazine and not to defend lawsuits. There was not any argument about that. And since the idea of the newsmagazine was to cover the events of the previous seven days, the juxtaposition of NEWS plus WEEK logically gave me the name *Newsweek*.

When I got down to the actual business to working out the format of *Newsweek* I gave a lot of thought to making it a pocket-size periodical. The decisive arguments against it came from the advertising people and were of a technical character. Advertising run in Time could not be run in a pocket magazine without additional expense to the advertisers. Difficulties of setting up a rate structure that would make sense. Lack of display facilities, etc. Eventually I gave up the idea, although to this day, especially in view of what the Readers Digest has accomplished, I am not sure that I was right in doing so. And so it happened that *Newsweek* became the same size as *Time* and for much the same reasons that Times had become the same size as the Literary Digest.

In considering a second newsmagazine, the question of the format was governed by the size and departmentalization was implicit in the concept - any concept - of a newsmagazine. But whereas Time was rigidly departmentalized, each department having a more or less fixed position, it was intended that *Newsweek* would be departmentalized more fluidly on a news importance basis. It did not seem to me to be necessary to go to extreme measures or to invent new means of presenting the news merely to make a superficial difference between the two news magazines. Newspapers are mostly much of a size and achieve physical differences through the use of type and editorial differences through the pursuit of different policies. And so it would be with two newsmagazines.

In synthesis a newsmagazine is a weekly newspaper in a more convenient size. Historically, there was nothing new then, nor is there now, in a weekly news report other than its format and application to modern requirements. There were weekly newspapers before the advent of Time just as there are many newsmagazines after it. There is nothing exclusive or original in a weekly newspaper any more than there is in a daily, weekly or monthly newsmagazine.

I expected *Newsweek* to be different in character than *Time*. I planned it that way. And I was not disappointed. I expected it to be much more accurate and even here I was not entirely disappointed. Although my ideas and aspirations were never to be fully realized, I was to become conscious that they were working for us in the steady progress we were to make. And my judgment was to be amply confirmed by our circulation record and what our circulation analysis revealed. We were to build up a solid *Newsweek* public.

In the early days, I based my reasoning on the realities of newspaper competition. If there was room for several newspapers in almost any big city in the United States all dealing with the same commodity (news), and literally thousands throughout the world, it did not require much imagination to visualize the profitable existence of two newsmagazine in the United States. Moreover, it seemed to me that competition in the business of weekly news presentation would expand the market for newsmagazines, which has been the case. It was just as obvious then as it is today with the benefits of hindsight. I believe that *Newsweek* has played its part in Time's stupendous success, and vice versa.

Briton Hadden died of a streptococcus infection in 1929. It is sad to think that if penicillin had been discovered at that time, he might have lived to enjoy the fruits of his labors and his remarkable aptitudes.

It was only late in the following year that I began to think actively and more or less continuously about the publication of another newsmagazine. I was fortunate in discovering that Winston Starling Childs Jr., who had married a first cousin of my wife, was every bit as much interested and just as enthusiastic as I was in and about my plans. We met frequently to discuss the project and I received very considerable encouragement from him. So much so, over the years ahead, that Winky, as his many friends affectionately knew him, is certainly to be regarded as the Uncle of *Newsweek*.

Aside from the money he personally invested and the far greater sums he directly and indirectly influenced, he was indefatigable in his efforts to assist me, sometimes with good ideas of his own, and always ready to do anything within his powers when asked, even to the point of personal inconvenience. He got every single member of his immediate family to subscribe to the stock of the new magazine, gave me introductions to some of his Yale classmates and induced his father to do likewise. When in later years successive increases in capital were required, Wink and his family were over prompt in taking up their agreed allotment, and on occasion the allotments of others, the defaulters. No man ever had a more faithful friend.

My conversations with Winky and many others continued sporadically throughout 1931 and it was only in the following year that the die was cast. Up to this time, I had had to proceed cautiously and carefully on my own time which meant in the evenings and during week-ends. There were a great many more factors to be considered and decided than I had previously imagined. The most obvious of these: Who were to be the editor, the business, circulation and advertising managers? In other words how and where was I to find the indispensable key personnel? Although jobs were scarce in those days, it was not an easy task for me. I did not have a wide circle of friends I could call on to help me. I had not been to school or college in the United States and therefore did not have a pool of classmates whom I could consult. I had in fact only been in the United States for nine years and many of my friends were to be counted on the staff of Time and while some of them were willing to help with advice which I did not solicit, there was no thought or possibility of any of them joining my venture. The taboo was established on morale as well as practical ratiocination. Despite all this handicap, the actual business of getting a staff together proved far less formidable than I had imagined. The cooperation, some of it from unexpected quarters, was total.

And there was the primary question of money. How much? Where from? How? The prospect of raising the large amount of initial capital required appeared at the time nothing short of foreboding to all concerned, except myself. I guess just blind faith in what I was doing carried me through to eventual success. Even in this respect reality was to prove far easier than the prospect for reasons I shall go into later on.

A host of other problems would follow or proceed the financial considerations, such as the definition of policy in its final terms, the actualization of the format, the choice of the printer and his location, who was to supply the paper, calculation of the results we expected over the first two years to a projected break-even point, and a great many others to which exact answers and best estimates had to be found before the prospectus could be written.

Overshadowing all these cerebrations was the supreme psychological doubt posed by the times. This was the year of presidential elections less than three years after the great Stock Market crash of 1929. The Dow Jones averages were at or close to their nadir, Franklin D. Roosevelt was addressing his fellow citizens and friends throughout the land preaching a new deal. It was the year of the Albert H. Wiggin scandal and the resultant wave of distrust in even the strongest banking institutions. People were frightened. Many were on the verge of starvation if not actually starving.

On the face of the situation, it looked about the most in-auspicious time to start a new enterprise, and for the majority of new ventures it undoubtedly was. My own thoughts were that the very gravity of the economic situation favored the foundation of a new journalistic undertaking. It seemed to me, and I suppose in retrospect it must have appeared to most thinking people, that the United States would have to undergo some heroic operation if the country were to be put on its feet again. No same person could doubt that it would be saved, though it is easy to say so now, but how the salvation was to be affected was one of the most disputatious questions of the day. My theory was that the very measures that would have to be taken would affect the lives of individual citizens as they had not been affected since the Civil War, and perhaps more momentously, for better or for worse, and certainly with equal intimacy. I figured a priori that the volume of news and its impact upon the public would increase and with it the demand for coherent news analysis. I was of course making a prima facie case for the launching in the midst of chaos of a new newsmagazine.

I could not proceed on the basis of my own opinions no matter how much I believed in them. To make additionally certain that I was not doing some highly speculative wishful thinking, I went to great pains to sound out the opinions and obtain the advice of a relatively considerable number of people whose views I could trust. Among these were several bankers, industrialists, brokers, lawyers and a fair selection of executive businessmen. In addition to this, we circularized 1,000 businessmen in New York, Chicago and Philadelphia, as well as directors of large corporations, automobile executives, doctors, ministers and educators.

The response was encouraging. Twenty-one percent answered, a very high return, and of these 54% were in favor of the type of newsmagazine we were advocating. Although they were not asked if they judged the time auspicious to start a new magazine, the implication was that they did. I do not now have the feeling that I got a majority opinion either pro or con. If there was a majority opinion then it was from people who admitted they had none. The people who were against the project per se were the most vehement in their denunciation of it. Some thought I was just plain crazy to think about it and told me bluntly that they would not think of investing in it at such a time and did not think anyone else would. Still others advised me to wait for the results of the forthcoming elections. I was able to persuade some of them that the times were in our favor, only to have them come up with a lot of other conditions they thought mattered still more. A few of them, and very important people among them, agreed fully with me. There was not any consensus. In the end I decided to go ahead on the theory that if I could raise the funds that in itself would be my best vindication.

Chapter Three

Staffing Up

Having made this decision I went to work to organize the venture. At the time, I was working in the Sunday Department of the New York Times under that master rewrite specialist Lester Martel. If Lester could be said to have a right hand man, that man was Samuel T. Williamson. He was the only man on the Sunday staff who could come close to rewriting an article the way Martel wanted it done. No small achievement in itself, because I sometimes thought that Lester himself did not know what he wanted. Sam was my direct opposite in temperament: equably calm, methodical and patient. If I remember correctly he had been with The New York Time for some thirteen years before I started to talk to him of my plans. Sam, ever courteous and cautious, listened to me long, often and silently. I kept after him perseveringly because I was convinced that he would be the ideal editor of the newsmagazine that was to be called *Newsweek*.

I never thought of Sam as a brilliant character and he did not become a brilliant editor. I felt that he had qualities that more than compensated for such deficiency. He was above all sound and possessed a keen sense of what was newsworthy in a panoramic sense. He knew what he wanted but was not always successful in getting it from others. He had excellent judgment and was happy in his choice of some brilliant writers some of whom have become outstandingly successful in a variety of journalistic fields. But he was too easy going, too kind. Rather than displease his staff he would himself rewrite an offending article, which sometimes had the opposite effect from that which he intended, annoying the author more deeply. His was a pleasant and unruffled personality but not a dominant one, and it seemed to me that his lack of authority which was perhaps his chief handicap, led him to unnecessary overwork and its consequent physical fatigue. Moreover, he found the exigencies of literary compression difficult of execution, sometimes falling into the use of barbarisms committed by Time, which I was anxious to avoid, all for the sake of effecting an unsuitable condensation. Sam was brilliant, however, in one respect: ideas, provided they were his own and he could translate them to paper himself. When it came to ideas agreed upon in conference he was not so fortunate in getting them executed by others, and I frequently felt a sense of disappointment in the results. All this is of course empiric. When I was talking to Sam about joining the venture I considered that I could not find a better nor a sounder man for the job and I have nothing to retract from that statement. And I can further state and take great pride in saying it that Sam was an integral part of *Newsweek*, a kingpin, and that under me he would always have had a trusted and honorable position on its staff. His subsequent dismissal by Malcolm Muir was ignoble, unjust and inexcusable for reasons that are very well known to me.

In the early days on Newsweek, Sam was a good counselor to me and made allowances for my excesses of temperament, knowing that my intentions were to seek the best for the welfare of the magazine. The fact that I was at times too outspoken, caustic and bad tempered undoubtedly led some people to think that Sam and I did not get along very well. For my part, nothing is farther from the truth.

If I had my own evaluation of Sam, and I obviously had, having known and worked with him for many years, I nevertheless based my judgment on his record. To be the right-hand man of a personality as positive and as complex as that of Lester Markel called for sterling qualities of judgment, tact, devotion and literary ability. One might agree with Markel, and some people did, I think, or one might disagree with him, and many people did, I know, but there is no gainsaying the fact that he had good judgment and considerable competence as a critic. His record on The New York Times is sufficient proof of that, even taking into consideration its nepotistic tendencies.

Markel had many other good qualities not the least of which was a nice discernment of the human element that made up his staff. I know that I am still proud of having once been associated with him. He knew how to get the best out of every one of us, his best of course, and he was extremely patient and persistent in getting it. To have worked even moderately successfully under Markel was a trial and a test the survival of which bespoke considerable individual merit. That Sam was the chief and the most venerable of Markel's disciples was enough to recommend him to me.

I never expected it would be easy, quite the contrary, to persuade Sam to sever his long-time allegiance to The New York times. At times I did not think I was going to succeed. Certainly the salary I was able to offer him was not an inducement. I still do not know what swayed his decision finally, although I have a pretty good idea that his wife, Cora, had something to do with it. In the end, after a siege of months, during which his enthusiasm for the new magazine perceptibly mounted, he agreed to become Newsweek's first editor. It was a large and serious decision for him to make and it took a great deal of faith and courage. Sam Williamson deserves a place of high honor in the annals of Newsweek.

A good, experienced business manager never crossed my vision, unfortunately, and it was impossible to go after one with the kind of money I would have to offer. Men with general business knowledge presented themselves, but none with specialized knowledge of the business. It was perhaps an error of judgment not to have accepted the services of one of these. At the time, I felt that I could do the job myself, never dreaming that I was taking much too big a load on my shoulders.

It was altogether a different matter with an advertising manager. He was the man we would have to depend on to administer our principal money-making department. Almost all of the advertising salesmen I had known who were personal friends of mine, were by that time occupying executive posts on various publications mostly put out by Time Inc. Aside from my friendship with these men and the esteem in which I held some of them, I felt, for a variety of reasons, most of all the pecuniary one, that I could not approach any of them. I was fully aware that between them they knew almost everyone worth knowing in the advertising world, but I do not recall seeking or receiving advice from any of them, probably for fear on both sides that our motives might be and probably would have been misunderstood. What I had to do seemed almost impossible, even taking into consideration widespread unemployment: find an experienced and successful advertising manager or salesman ambitious enough to risk a good position for less immediate money on the gamble that an interest in a new venture would pay off in the long run. I eventually found such a man in Edward L. Rea.

Ted, as we all knew him, had been the star salesman of Parents Magazine and was at the time selling an appreciable percentage of that magazine's space. In consequence of this he did not feel that his talents were being sufficiently recognized and compensated. For this reason he was ready to listen to me. Ted was as bald as a bean, with an engaging personality, a good sense of humor, polite to a fault, and seemed to know what he was talking about. I say seemed advisedly because what I did not know at the time is that many a good advertising salesman makes a poor advertising director. That proved to be unfortunately the case with Ted. At the time I was very much impressed with him, and I well remember that Winky Childs was too. Not only did he have a good record and a pleasing presence, but he was the only member of Newsweek's staff to quit his moderately lucrative job there and then and to share the risks involved in the organization of the new newsmagazine and to help in the raising of the capital, at which he was remarkably unsuccessful. Ted is therefore to be considered a co-founder of Newsweek. To give him full credit, he worked hard and cooperated fully with me. Together we made a trip in his automobile that took us from New England to New York, Pennsylvania, Indiana, Ohio, Michigan and Illinois. Only in Chicago, as I remember it, did we hit pay dirt but not much of it. The trip had cost us personally a fair percentage of the money we had raised for the venture.

As I have said, it was one thing to have been a successful advertising salesman and quite another to become a successful advertising manager especially of a new periodical. Ted, unfortunately for all concerned, did not have what it took and when that became apparent there was little I knew how to do to help him. He was responsible, though, for the happiest Christmas I remember when he proudly announced that we had some one thousand (or some such number) pages of advertising on our books for 1934. Had that been true, or even substantially realized, Newsweek would have turned the corner in that year as originally scheduled. It was not true, far from it; the so-called orders were merely rate-holders subject to confirmation which never came or came in minimal amounts. This was by no means Ted's fault alone. He had done a magnificent job of convincing some imposing accounts to protect themselves against probable rate increases in the coming year. The fact that nothing like the then expected volume of advertising was secured in 1934 was probably more my fault than is and equally the fault of the other directors, which will be fully discussed later on.

The important point for me, and for everyone else for that matter, and bitterly disappointing it was, was that Ted did not seem to have known what a rate-holder was and continued to treat them as realizable orders and to wax enthusiastic about them for a large part of the year. This may be unfair to Ted. Perhaps he did know what a rate-holder was. If he did, he most certainly did not succeed in convincing me and the rest of his co-directors. It was on the basis of these rate-holders that I was able to secure additional capital in 1934 and when the expected income did not materialize a very difficult situa-

tion was created. Although, as I have already said, the responsibility for this failure was not Ted's alone, he logically had to
bear the brunt of the criticism that followed. It was a melancholy disillusionment for me when I could not defend Ted
before the other directors and was forced ultimately to get his
resignation. There was no other way out. The future of the
magazine was at stake as it was to become at stake later on
with my "severance".

After Ted left Newsweek, I never heard from him again
and I hope that he harbors no bitterness against me for his
departure. What I did I had to do and I felt sincerely that it
was in the best interest of the magazine he had helped to
found. I learned afterward that Ted quit the advertising field
to study law and that he is now a successful practicing lawyer
in New York. More power to him.

The rest of the key staff and some of the editorial staff
appeared among the people who successfully helped with the
raising of funds. Foremost among them was Francis Dewitt
Pratt, known as Mooney because of his big round face, who
eventually became Newsweek's circulation manager. He knew
nothing about the intricate functions of a circulation department at the start and what he learned initially he learned from
me and Julian Watkins. Since neither Julian nor I were professional circulation men, it is small wonder that between us we
made mistakes. Serious and costly at the time, but insignificant
in a long-range plan. Mooney cooperated with me fully in
every sense of that adverb and was surely one of my most loyal

collaborators. When he left Newsweek, under circumstances of which I am still unaware, he was taken on by Roy Larsen of Time Inc. as a circulation executive. Roy was not a man to give a responsible position to anyone without thorough investigation and satisfaction. His appointment to a post of trust in the Time organization, it seems to me, measures the worth of the man in his professional capacity and at the same time justifies the immense faith in and my dependence on Mooney.

There is one other early Newsweeker, one among many, that I like to remember: Julian Watkins, who became Newsweek's first circulation chief and general promotion manager. Julian's forte was promotion and since he had a brilliant mind it was not surprising that he turned out some scintillating copy for the magazine. Appointed by Ted Rea, if my memory holds, he threw himself into the task of early organization and subsequent routine with rare verve. Unfortunately for us and like many people of his temperament, he was unstable and impatient and he did not stay with us very long. I seem to remember that we made some arms-length arrangement with him for future cooperation which did not work out. It was with real regret, no matter if I did put a different face on it at the time, that we saw him go.

Around this time, that is during the year 1932, I met Marvin Pierce, who was to play a decisive part in my subsequent fate. At this time, he was Vice President of the McCall Corporation, an engineer by profession and that time the executive responsible for the McCall printing plant in Dayton,

Ohio. Marvin was extraordinarily helpful to me often going out of his way to do me a favor, beyond the call of duty to McCall's, providing me with all the estimates I required and requested, which were considerable, and helping me with the problem of securing a good paper source. Afterward, when I checked the estimates he had supplied and obtained with those of other printers and paper manufacturers, and when all the surrounding factors had been taken into consideration, including those stemming from geographical location, the bids from McCall's and the suppliers suggested by Marvin were found to be by far the most attractive.

Chapter Four

Raising Capital

With part of the staff selected and compromised and a mass of complicated cost factors at hand, although there was no particular order involved between the two, it became possible for the first time to consider the additional information that would be required before the amount of initial capital needed could be calculated. And beyond this, there were other considerations to be taken into account. One was the $87,000 that Time had widely publicized as its original capital. I knew of course, or rather I had been reliably informed, that Time's original capital had been supplemented by a loan or loans of undetermined amounts as far as I was concerned.

The important point for me was that Time had reached a point on the basis of its original capital where loans had become a practical possibility. Obviously, it was good business to borrow rather than increase the capital stock. This factor was very certainly in my subconscious mind as I began to work on my estimates and I suppose I kept this knowledge as a sort

of an ace in the hole in case of necessity. In making my calculations, I was conscientiously resolved to establish a realistic
basis for future operations and to be rigorously governed by
it. That I did not succeed, and that nobody could have succeeded under the abnormal conditions that were to prevail, is
beside the point at this juncture. I could have set up big reserves to cover a host of contingencies, but to do so would
have defeated me at the start. What I had to figure was how
much I needed upon predetermined bases.

Obviously, I was going to need a great deal more than it
had taken Time to establish itself. For one thing it was impossible for me to put out a newsmagazine of the poor quality of
the first issues of Time to compete with the excellent quality
of Time in 1933. We had to have better paper and better printing and both cost far more than they did Time back in 1923.
The times were against us in that as well as in some other respects but in our favor in many others. Everybody was hungry
for business and jobs and because of this we were able to
make some good bargains. But quality was one of the things
with which we could not bargain. The same thing was true of
promotion materials, particularly direct mail for circulation
promotion. The editorial department would likewise cost
more for a number of different reasons, not the least of which
was that it took more people at better than average 1933 sala-
ries to turn out a newsmagazine fit to compete with Time in
1933.

Then there was the all-important price factor. Time with a relatively good volume of advertising would bulk well against a lean Newsweek which could not expect much advertising initially. On the face of it appeared crazy to sell Newsweek for $4 a year and 10 cents a single copy against $5 a year for Time and 15 cents a copy. When Luce heard of it, he was reported to me as having said, "That's strike one against him." Maybe he was right, but after the passage of more than 30 years I do not think so.

If the bulk argument was valid at that time, it was to become more so after we started publication, because Newsweek did not get anything like the volume, small though it was, of advertising we had hoped for. The $4 subscription and the 10 cent single copy price were adopted to overcome anticipated sales resistance. It was a psychological measure, to make the price differential another sales argument in favor of Newsweek. It was not intended to be a permanent measure but rather an expedient to get us going as quickly as possible. It would be altogether factitious to assert today a future rise in prices that would force us to a sharp upward revision of our subscription prices. I do not think that anyone, certainly no one connected with us, imagined that costs would soar to the extent they have, forcing a general upward trend in prices. I did feel though that there would come a time when Newsweek's volume would justify an increase to the Time level.

However, I had an overriding reason for fixing a low subscription and single copy price for Newsweek. Although some
of us thought that the bottom had been touched and that better times were just around the corner, a casual look at the economic wilderness was enough to convince the most blatant
optimist that there must be a severe shortage of cash money
in the people's pocket. Most of us indeed were feeling it. A
lower price was intended therefore to have a greater appeal to,
and a smaller drain on, the buying public whose slender resources were to become even slenderer in the immediate future. Not only this, but allied with it, was the argument of a
single coin transaction for newsstand sales. The chief expo-
nent of this argument was William Patrick Cashin,
Newsweek's first newsstand manager whose tenure of that office was to last for 33 years, and who had been recommended
to me by Mike Morrissy of the American News Company.
Mike never did a better turn for Newsweek. Bill's great energy
and his undisputed ability made his voice a potent force in our
councils and his opinion on this momentous matter, aside
from my own convictions, was enough to carry the argument
and to dissipate any doubt that may have been lurking around
the edges of it. Bill's paramount loyalty during most of his
working life has been total to Newsweek. I am proud to be
honored with his friendship to this day.

Thus it was the merchandising argument, plus the panic
economic condition of the country, plus the convenience of a
single coin newsstand sale that decided the price structure of

Newsweek. As I write these lines the single copy price of Newsweek has gone to 40 cents!

An analysis and comparison of Time's circulation price structure with that decided for Newsweek will show that our subscription price should have been $3.33 a year on the basis of the same 50% mark up from the subscription price to the annual single copy price for both magazines. This would seem to indicate a hidden and probably highly theoretical advantage for Newsweek; but practically, I think, its only utility is to indicate that I did not undercut Time solely for the sake of doing so, as has been suggested in some quarters. Newsweek's subscription price could have been arithmetically 50 cents lower if that had been the case.

Actually Newsweek's net paid circulation grew year by year over the next four years at a faster rate than Time's had done in its first four years. This growth was partly by design, partly from necessity, and to a great extent naturally. That it cost more, much more than was estimated, even relatively, does not detract from the indisputable fact that our circulation policy was successful and exceeded my best estimates. The higher cost of obtaining short-term subscriptions meant, it is true, that it would take us longer to assimilate them, which would in turn cost more money; but against that it can be said that every long-term subscription put on our books resulted in a profit large enough to make the total operation lucrative. That is an incontrovertible fact, despite my critics.

With the subscription price structure fixed, we went on to determine the advertising rate basis. Since this was outside my experience, at least more so than in other fields, I had little to do with it. Although Ted Rea's estimates were sharply at variance with the reality of them, I am inclined to think out of memory that they were closer to the truth than many of my own. But once the rates had been settled and the estimates made I was free to fit them into a budget that would dictate the amount of capital we should require.

As I have indicated before, if my estimates could have included provision for a more expert staff, ample allowance for advance publicity and with ample reserves to take care of budget deficiencies, we might have gone ahead more surely to a quicker success. I am still not prepared to say that we would have made better progress, because what happened to us in the first month of our existence might just as well resulted in a still greater loss of money through the negation of such publicity efforts. And what I shall call a deluxe program was entirely beyond our possibilities. Such a program would have cost perhaps a million dollars, or more, and I am quite sure, even at this distance, that we never could have raised such an amount of initial capital in such desperate times as these through which we were passing in 1932.

Hard and intelligent work is worth a lot of capital and that is what we had to contribute. Still, there is no doubt that with a bit more than ample capital, estimates being what they always are, our chances for quick success would have been magnified. Starling Childs told me afterward that in the public utility industry he doubled the estimated time and quadrupled the original estimated cost and even at that prayed for the best. To have done that in our case would have called for a capital of $3,500,000 on the basis of the same estimated income prorated over four years. I do not suppose for one minute that even Mr. Childs would have been interested in putting up money for Newsweek on that basis. No doubt too that a large capitalization would have breathed a spirit of confidence into the whole enterprise, the kind of confidence that would attract and hold advertisers. That sort of set-up would, in my case, have saved me ultimately from the vicious effects of the irresponsibility of my board of directors. And of course my own inability to deal effectively with it. But it was not in the cards.

When I had my estimated controlling figures, I made three budgets: the first on a vary fancy basis, the second on what I thought we could reasonably expect and the third the worst that I thought could happen to us. None of them was any good. The first just staggered me. The second was close enough to our potentialities to invite further study. The third meant that we would be doomed before we got started. But in the end, plan number two was adopted, with some revisions, and even it proved the truth of Mr. Child's observations that estimates are notoriously deceptive and unreliable. Certainly mine were and I had to revise them the hard way.

The philosophy which governed my calculations was rigidly based on making circulation eventually pay for itself. Once I had adopted the rule I was controlled by it and I never deviated from it, with one small exception, until the end of my administration. Once circulation was regarded as an expense, the whole cost of it, or close thereto, would fall on advertising income, with a drastic effect on net profit. Moreover, the means chosen to make circulation a paying business also gave us the means of measuring the success of the venture more or less continuously and with a high degree of accuracy through careful and systematic subscription analysis. Thus if short-term subscriptions on our books were converted into long-term subscriptions there would be a fair presumption that a given number of people were willing to pay $4 a year, a step-up of $3 from the $1 introductory offer, for the magazine and for only one reason: that they liked it. According to my way of looking at it the real test would come a year later when it would become possible to discover if our regular readers continued to like it.

Obviously it would be several years before we could build up a backlog of long-term subscriptions on a broad enough basis to carry the circulation department, especially in view of our subsequent decision to grow more rapidly in order to provide a more attractive and profitable advertising unit. That decision could not be made, however, until we knew through analysis if we were in fact creating a Newsweek public. Until we reached a break-even point we would have for many years to come a preponderant number of short-term offers on our books at a net loss for every single one of them. Originally we had hoped that at conversion the resultant income would be enough to pay for the entire operation to that point. This did not happen, not because our conversion rate was low, but because the return on our direct mail efforts was not what we expected it to be. In other words the cost of putting a net paid short-term subscription on our books was much higher than we had estimated, owing to a variety of reasons.

After conversion we still had a small net loss per thousand long-term subscriptions on our books secured in this way. We estimated correctly that an extension of these subscriptions for an equal period would give us a net profit for the transaction viewed as a whole. The trouble was that the profit was not big enough, but it was a profit. Prorated it was not enough to pay for the total cost of the circulation department. In practice we discovered there was a third stage that we had not suspected. Two-year readers of Newsweek renewed in a surprising number. This could only mean that our readers felt that the magazine was indispensable to them. The resultant profit, prorated, gave us what we were after: a profitable net paid circulation.

All this was in the future. What I had calculated might work out better or it might work out worse. If it worked out reasonable well, we should have an infallible index of our reader interest. We should then have created our own public on a paying basis. If it worked out badly, we should have painfully acquired the knowledge that there was not any place in the public consciousness for a second newsmagazine.

Budgets for the first two years complied for the purposes of the prospectus relied upon a net 2% return on direct mail circulation promotion and a volume of advertising rising to 10 pages per issue. We did not get either. We had estimated a loss of $130,000 for the first year and in fact it was not far off that figure at the end of 1933. The profit of $160,000 for the second year became a loss of more than that amount for two primary reasons: 1) the conditions under which we were operating were not conducive to the results we had estimated; 2) the bases used for estimating the budget, especially for the second year, had to be modified because (a) the results for the first year forced a revision and (b) we had raised our sights and were aiming at a higher circulation. The second year's budget is not therefore a criterion.

Looking backward, I can see quite clearly, what was by no means evident at the time, that I had underestimated the cost of the new program. My recollection is that our net return from direct mail was a little better than half what I had expected and estimated. This meant that every short-term subscription had cost us the double of what I had forecast. I knew this of course, but what I had not paid sufficient attention to was the cost of obtaining the subscriptions we had failed to secure as the result of our lower return. As far as I recall I had not figured and reserve for such a purpose. What influenced me in those far off days was the knowledge that we had a sound indication of an economic basis for our circulation promotion, despite higher costs. Though a more rapid growth than I had planned would certainly cost more money, it was just as certain that each dollar we invested in our circulation would eventually come back to us with a profit. And, after all, the objective of increasing our net paid circulation was to attract more advertising, and the more advertising we got, the less the drain on capital.

In writing this memoir, I am not trying to whitewash myself or to defend myself against the criticisms I know about or still less against those I know exist without knowing what they are. I am writing for the record and in writing it I am well aware that I was too optimistic in making the various estimates I was called on to make during my administration of Newsweek, especially in the early days. Even if the year 1933 had been a year of recovery, I should have still been overconfident in my estimates. In fact, I was only to be right about them in one respect, that of the public acceptance of the second newsmagazine. It did not come spontaneously but slowly and certainly.

Long before this I had quit my job on The New York Times in order to devote my whole time and attention to the organization and financing of Newsweek. No doubt it was a bold step for me to take with a wife and a new born son and heir. The risk was a calculated one and as far as the foundation of Newsweek was concerned and it worked out to that extent.

It was a risk moreover that should entitle me to a great deal more consideration than I was to get and a risk that none of the subsequent proprietors and administrators were called upon to make. At that time, it was for me a case of nothing venture, nothing win. Helen gave me total support. We worked out a budget of sorts to the end of 1932 including anticipated expenses for the initial expenses of the "brain child". My wife's family was aghast at my temerity, having evidently forgotten that America is the land of opportunity. But once I was set and on my way they were loyal and as helpful as they could be. I was taking Briton Haddon's advice literally.

Several men offered their services to me to help raise the initial capital on the basis that if successful they would each get a job on the magazine. Although I had qualms about such arrangements, it was a case of not leaving a stone unturned. Chief of these men were Bob McMahon, who became one of the first members of the editorial staff; Orville Prescott, through his brother Hank, who became Newsweek's first book reviewer and whose name is now nationally known as the principal book reviewer for The New York Times; and Francis Pratt who eventually was to become Newsweek's circulation manager. No doubt I was exceedingly lucky in the choice of these colleagues.

On March 28, 1932, I opened an escrow account with the New York Trust Company under the terms of which the amounts deposited there under were to be released to a company to be formed by me prior to January 1, 1933 for the purposes of publishing "a magazine". The agreement called for a capital of 5,000 shares of $3 Cumulative Preference Stock without par value and 15,000 shares of Common Stock also without par value. One share of preferred and one share of common were to be sold as a unit for $50. In the event that a minimum amount of $200,000 was not raised prior to the end date, the amounts deposited in the escrow account were to be returned to the depositors. Winky Childs was the first depositor.

By early summer we had about half the money we were after deposited, with enough promises for the rest and still some others considering a subscription,. We had had some experience with promises. The difficulty with them was to get the money deposited in the bank. And for this reason and also to get a better geographical distribution of capital, Ted Rea and I decided to make a trip to the Mid-West in search of new prospects. It was early that summer when Franklin D. Roosevelt had just been or was about to be nominated for the Presidency by the Democratic Party that we set out on a 2,000-mile trip from points west. We left Hartford, Conn. One bright early morn, as I recollect it, armed with a packet of introductions. Our route went through Binghampton and Elmira, New York, Warren, Penn. down to Pittsburgh and on up to Youngstown and Cleveland. From Cleveland we went to Akron, thence to Sandusky, Toledo and Detroit. After a stay of a couple of days or so in Detroit we went on to Chicago by way of Jackson and South Bend, returning by much of the same route. We were gone about a month and had very little to show for it except promises. And if all of them had been kept we would have raised half a million dollars long before the end of the year. As it turned out the expense of the trip bore a high ratio to the amount of money we eventually collected from it.

Later on Helen and I were to make a special trip to Cincinnati to see Junius (Junky) Fleischmann at his invitation. We had met before in New York at one of the innumerable parties given by Bill Carr. This must have been soon after the Lindbergh baby kidnapping, for when we get there the drive to Junky's house was full of humps, which had the effect of slowing down traffic to about one mile an hour and was designed as a protection for his children. We only stayed for a weekend and were treated like a couple of visiting royalty. On the Sunday, Junky and his wife gave us a smorgasbord of gigantic proportions, held on top of the indoor swimming pool which had been boarded over for the event, and to which half the countryside had been invited, or so it seemed. It was an unforgettable luncheon for us. We departed for New York that same afternoon by train, the richer for a subscription of $1,000 to the capital of Newsweek. Not as much as we had hoped for, and obtained at a high cost to us, but we had had a wonderful visit.

When Ted and I got back from out trip, somewhat disappointed but far from dispirited, we threw ourselves into the fight for Newsweek once more in the certain knowledge that most of the money would come from New York and nearby states. And so it did. By the first of December we had something like three quarters of it. Soon afterward we got to the 90% point and we were beginning to get very nervous when Winky Childs offered to put up the remainder if it became necessary. Fortunately it did not become necessary, for by the end of the year we had gone well beyond the stipulated minimum.

Our stockholders included at that time and later beside the Childs and Cheney families, Henry Prescott, Wilton Lloyd-Smith, Howell van Gerbig, Junius Fleischmann, John Hay Whitney, Paul Mellon, M. Roland Harriman and Nelson Rockefeller. At the time, Nelson was peddling space in the far from completed Rockefeller Center. I made a bargain with him the result of which he subscribed $100 to the stock of Newsweek Inc. and Newsweek became the first tenant of Rockefeller Center at an attractive rental.

With Newsweek Inc. formed at the end of 1932 and the escrow money finally transferred to the credit of its bank account in the New York Trust Company, we were ready to start operations. Sam Williamson resigned from The New York Times on my 37th birthday, January 3, 1933, almost ten years to a day since I had first landed in the United States to work for Time.

Chapter Five

The First Issue

A tremendous amount of work lay ahead of us before we would be ready to publish volume 1, number 1 of Newsweek. We already had the nucleus of an editorial staff from the start, but there were a number of others to be interviewed and hired. There was no difficulty in finding them and for this reason we were able to pick and choose with admirable results. Ted Rea was busy organizing his advertising department and to appoint representatives in key cities restricted to Cleveland, Detroit and Chicago at that time. Bill Cashin, who had been working without pay prior to the incorporation, was not only busy organizing his own department but, as usually with him, was helpful generally and generously in every direction in which he could find an outlet for his abundant energies. I was fortunate in finding a good accountant and together we set up a control system that I have been told endured in part for more than a quarter of a century. I also had to instruct Mooney Pratt in the mysteries of circulation in his capacity as acting circulation manager under Julian Watkins and to plan our first direct mail campaign with both of them. On top of this I had to set up our lines of communication with the McCall printing plant in Dayton, Ohio, in which I was ably and generously assisted by Marvin Pierce, and to contract for the initial paper supply in which Marvin was also a great help.

Everybody wanted something or other and I soon found myself faced with stacks of requests from each department which I had to approve or disapprove. In that first week it became evident that I had got myself a seven-day a week job, and so it proved to be over the next four years, with very few respites, with the hours per day always seeming to grow longer. But no man was better served by a more loyal and con-secrated staff. And the burden I had assumed would have been far heavier had it not been for the intelligent, capable and devoted services of my secretary, Mildred Haibel. Able Haibel, as she was affectionately known to all of us, stayed with me until the end, through the good days and the bad ones, always with the same undiminished devotion. It was impossible with such people around me not to feel full of enthusiasm and faith in the success of Newsweek.

How it was managed I have not any clear idea, but on January 14, less than two weeks after our start, we produced our first dummy. With all the other things we had to do it still seems like a miracle. While nobody was very pleased with it, it was a necessary and important first step to train us for the procedure we would have to follow with increased efficiency for every single week of our existence. We took more time over the second dummy, dated February 10. It was a better job and we all were a bit more satisfied with it. Moreover the means utilized to get it to press were much improved. Great credit for that was due to Sam Williamson and his able managing editor Harding Mason. We were now ready to go ahead with the first issue Volume No. 1, No. 1 of Newsweek.

On the occasion of the publication of the first issue I sent a letter to Henry R. Luce and received one from him. These letters are no longer in my possession and I therefore cannot quote them here. Mine to him must have stated the hope that he would have taken some pride in the fact that an old Timer was starting the second newsmagazine. Of his reply to me I have not the slightest recollection. Thirty-three years later I heard from the editor of the history of Time that this exchange of letters is to appear in that history. I asked him if he would be so kind to send me photostatic copies of them but never received a reply, much less the copies.

The first issue of Newsweek appeared with seven pictures on the cover, the idea being to illustrate the main event of each day of the news week covered, thereby lending an explanation of the title of the magazine. While the idea was theoretically justifiable, it was not practical, for several diverse reasons. Moreover, Bill Cashin began to fight against its continuance on the ground that it was not attractive in a merchandising sense and that he was having difficulty in getting display for the magazine on the newsstands. I was loathe to give it up on the score that we should find the means of improving it. We did not succeed, partly because of the poor quality of news pictures in those days and partly because the idea was not practical on a cover of our size. Eventually I had to admit myself defeated and with the issue of June 16, 1934, the seven picture covers were discontinued and replaced by a single picture cover. Bill Cashin began to get better displays and his judgment was to be fully vindicated later on by better results.

The publication of the first issue of Newsweek coincided with the beginnings of the banking panic that was to lead to the national bank moratorium of March 5. Newsweek's third issue was dated March 3. I don't suppose, even if we had it within our power to try that we could have picked a worse time in which to launch a new magazine. How much it cost us in terms of the dissipation of our precious capital cannot of course be measured. At that particular time we were not aware of what the collapse of our financial institutions was doing to us. We knew it was bad but we were not to know how bad for several months when it became apparent that our initial capitalization was doomed. With the whole nation in a state of shock it was not surprising that our first direct mailing was away off from our expectations; but since it was not a large mailing we had not any cause to be unduly concerned. And we still had but little idea of the newsstand sales for the first issue. Our crisis, or rather crises, were in the future.

A light note was injected into this somber picture, at the time on the humorous side. A friend of mine, a Vice President of a large corporation in New York, phoned me on Monday, March 6 (I have never forgotten the date) to say he had seen the crisis coming, which was not too difficult with banks closing right and left all over the country, and had withdrawn a large amount of money the week before. "Tom," he said to me in substance, "if you need anything up to $100,000, call on me." I wonder what he would have said if I had called on him, and I wonder still more if he would have ever made the offer if he had known the extent of our capitalization. Fortunately, we did not need to avail ourselves of this offer. Whenever I think of this man I remember his pleasing and comforting gesture.

Three months after the bank moratorium it became evident that we would not have enough money to reach the objectives for which I had budgeted. As was to be expected, although we did not, final figures for the first newsstand sales were bad, far below my estimates. Our short-term offers (20 weeks for $1) were a little better than half what I had hoped for, discounting the results of the moratorium week, and a little less than half, including that week's results. Collections were slow to bad and accounted for the low net paid direct mail results to a fairly a large extent. Advertising revenue was away off, too, from our modest expectations.

I began to worry about the money situation. Obviously we were going to need more of it. I talked to Winky about what was happening to us. I said that sooner or later we were going to be obliged to look for new sources of money, for I did not think we could go back to our original stockholders less than a year after we had started publication, especially as we had not as yet proved anything. Winky's reaction was characteristic. He produced some new prospects. I went to them and was successful beyond my best expectations. Thus the situation, which had not become anything like critical in terms that it was to later on, was relieved and we had enough money in hand and in sight to last until we should surely have some proof that we were on the right track.

At this point I gradually became aware that even this new money would not be enough to finance us into the black. And from then on I began to think of a basis upon which I could go back to the stockholders for more money. There was one possible basis and that was to prove that the public we were reaching liked and enjoyed the magazine and for that we should have to wait.

By the fall of the year we were beginning to get reliable results of our efforts to induce our trial subscribers, those who had paid $1 for short term subscription, to pay $4 for an annual subscription. This was the first objective and the decisive test. It was with well-nigh indescribable joy and relief that we learned that our conversion rate from short to long terms was almost as high as we had hoped for in our estimates, proof positive that our readers liked the magazine. Before I could go back to our stockholders we still had to know how many readers paying the full price would renew, and for that we would have to wait until 1934. Joy and relief, but soon clouded over, for the cost of securing our short terms was nearly double what I had forecast. This sharp increase in our costs became apparent to us when we were obliged to mail twice in order to obtain more or less the number of subscriptions I had budgeted, which was obligatory in view of our circulation guarantee to advertisers.

And newsstand sales continued to be low. Bill Cashin would not let me cut the newsstand order because he was having a hard enough time as it was to get display on the newsstand. This meant that newsstand sales were a continuing drain on our resources week after week. Relatively this was not a serious matter, or I should have had no option but to reduce the order. Also, on top of everything else, advertising sales continued to be far, very far, below our budgeted requirements. This was pretty much our situation at the end of 1933.

By Christmastime, however, the prospects for 1934 brightened perceptively – or so it seemed – with Ted's forecast of advertising income. That and the knowledge that our conversion rate was holding up. Although Ted's forecast was never to be realized it was undoubtedly a positive element in helping to get together the additional capital we were going to need. Early in 1934, in agreement with Winky Childs, I called a meeting of the Board of Directors and treated that meeting as a ways and means committee. The directors were in complete agreement with my views, but thought it would be better to get some new people into the picture before we went back to the original stockholders. This was reasonable enough and was actually the way in which I was to meet Wilton Lloyd-Smith, who was to be my mentor, savior and guardian angel for two whole years.

What I wanted from the directors was money, if only enough to tide us over until we could go after the $250,000 I had asked for, and I had asked for it by a fixed date. When I did not get it by that time, our situation began to grow desperate. I could not even get the Board together again. When I was talking of going over the head of the directors to the stockholders, Winky invited me to lunch. We had it in nearby Tony's restaurant, at that time his only restaurant. I used to have my lunches there and often my dinners and frequently saw some of the famous members of the staff of the New Yorker. Tony and his wife became good friends, a friendship that has lasted to this day. Every time he sees me, though the gaps are years apart, he greets me with outstretched arms. "Ha! The founder of Newsweek."

The most memorable lunch of all was this one with Wink in the early spring of 1934. My spirits were at an all-time low and with the passage of time I do not remember the conversation except that it was certainly about Newsweek. What I do remember was the check for $25,000 that Wink handed me at the end of the meal – "just to tide us over until we can get our big money." No check has ever looked so big to me in my life nor more gratefully received and it did just what it was intended to do.

Wilton Lloyd-Smith lived two doors away from us on Gracie Square in an enormous duplex penthouse overlooking the East River. On my first visit he received me in his private library, the walls of which were covered by well burnished pigskin. We had an immediate meeting of the minds. I liked him at first sight and I felt that he liked me. He became a very good friend to me until almost the end when he turned against me for reasons which even now I find impossible to analyze. He was a rich man in his own right and he had married a Marjorie Fleming, reputed to be the largest lady preferred stockholder of U.S. Steel. He was a lawyer and one of the senior partners of a large and well known law firm in Wall Street. I had the feeling that he was not particularly active outside the administration of his wife's huge fortune, which probably kept him busy enough.

As was to be the case a little later on when I had my only meeting with President Roosevelt, Wilton opened his dealings with me by a long and virulent attack on Harry Luce. Wilton's detestation of Luce was no doubt the motive that induced him to talk with me in the first place and to join with me in the second place. Looking backward, I think I should be more generous than I am toward Harry and give him a big vote of thanks for his unintentional aid. I no longer remember the details behind Wilton's loathing of Harry Luce, except that it concerned the million dollars that Wilton arranged for Harry to enable him to buy the bulk of the Time shares in the Briton Hadden estate. As I recall Wilton's tirade, it had something to do with an option that Harry promised Wilton to buy a given number of Times shares at a fixed price. Beyond that, I remember nothing, most probably because it did not directly concern me. Either the option did not materialize, or was not for the number of shares agreed upon, or was not for the stipulated price. I do remember thinking, either at the time or soon afterward, that as a lawyer he might be expected to take better care of himself. What I recall vividly is Wilton's fury at Luce whom he abused by every conceivable derogatory epithet he could think of, and accused him inter alia of base ingratitude toward his benefactors, particularly those who had paid for his education at Hotchkiss and Yale while his father was a poor missionary in China, where Luce was born. I had no way of knowing, nor was I interested in knowing, the merits involved in this diatribe against Luce. Later on I got to know that the benefactor named by Wilton had been a classmate of Harry's father at Yale and also of one of Helen's uncles who confirmed that the benefactor had in fact financed Harry's education. What Wilton had to do with this, if anything, I likewise do not remember. What griped Wilton excessively was Luce's ingratitude toward his benefactor whose family he was charged with having basely attacked in an early issue of Fortune, much to that family's disgust. Knowing Luce as well as I do all this still does not surprise me. I find it entirely in character and conforms to my private opinion of him.

That Wilton felt himself seriously affronted, aggrieved and injured there was no doubt; for he referred to Luce afterward frequently and always in terms of opprobrium.

It is only fair to say that Wilton was not a very stable character. He was ever very full of himself, what he had done and how he had done it. He had an excellent and impressive presence, when he was not showing off, and could be extremely pleasant and persuasive when he wanted to be. Like most rich men he was impatient of criticism. Beneath apparent joviality, he was acutely sensitive and was often caustic to the point of rudeness behind a semi-jocose manner. He had a beautiful estate on Long Island's north shore, next door to Marshall Field, and lived a life of luxury. He had I do not know how many automobiles, including a ramshackle Rolls Royce which was his pride and joy. He was full of all the wonderful parties he had given and attended and was ever looking for a new one. And why not. Even the rich have their rights and their faults. One of the latter was to buy a milk cow. Either he did not bother to have the milk pasteurized, or it was done improperly a result of which he contracted undulating fever. It is my opinion that this disease unbalanced his mind and accounted for his subsequent suicide. He shot himself in his lovely library in his luxurious Gracie Square apartment.

Wilton helped me immediately with my financial problems, both he and Marjorie subscribing $50,000 of the $250,000 I was after. He went with me to see some of our most important stockholders and within a week to ten days I had all the money in the bank. As I had invited Wilton to become a director and he had accepted, I revamped the Board which if my memory holds consisted of Wilton Lloyd-Smith, S. Winston Child Jr., Howell van Gerbig, Ward Cheney, Edward L. Rea and myself as chairman.

Chapter Six

Meetings with Remarkable Men

The publication business is built firmly on confidence and nothing engenders confidence better than success and a fat bank account. Failing these, no matter how sound the development of a new venture might be, the gossips got to work. Like hungry wolves that can smell blood miles away, these chatterers could not only smell trouble in the making but could disseminate the news overnight. Since every publication is scrambling for its piece of the advertising pie, it is a dog eat dog proposition. The rumor mongers were of course busy with us and from what I could gather over the grapevine we were expected to fold any day. No doubt our competition was happy to join the wolves. I mention this at this juncture because it was an element we had not counted on and explains to a degree why Ted Rea was unable to convert his rate holders into orders. We had to pay dearly for the loss of confidence in our future at that time and the resultant loss of our personal prestige was ultimately to eliminate Ted and later me.

The question of confidence was to loom large in the future of my relations with the Board of Directors. During the rest of my administration of Newsweek, I drummed it into the consciousness of my directors the absolute necessity of taking curative action well before the crisis appeared in order to avoid deleterious effects on advertising income. That I failed miserably in this respect I acknowledge. Had I been clairvoyant I could have avoided the troubles I was to encounter later on by putting our finances on a totally different basis. It was naturally in my interest, in the interest of all of us, to make a success on the least possible amount of capital and for this reason I admit I relied too heavily on the good will of my directors.

At all times I kept them fully informed concerning out operations. We held monthly meetings for that purpose. My directors would readily agree to suggested changes of policy, even in face of the information that such changes would cost more money, but they were not so ready to supply it or help provide it. They were past masters in the art of procrastination. Can't you get along with less? How much do you need until the end of the week, or month? This attitude could hardly have been more harmful to Newsweek and when I reproached them with it, as I often did, they did not like it which led to tactics of recrimination. In the end, of course, they got fed up with me accusing me of using the Board improperly as money raisers. This was a valid criticism, but when later on I wanted to recapitalize, I got divided support and much more opposition. And I failed totally to get the Board to recognize its own responsibility for our future recurring crises.

With circulation showing satisfactory results and the extra expense of securing short-term subscriptions taken care of, it was the lack of anticipated advertising income that was to be a drain on our resources. Ted was well aware of this toward the end of the year and we were both alarmed. Ted then suggested that it might be a good idea for me to take a swing around the advertising territory in which he was backed up by our representatives in Cleveland, Detroit and Chicago. There were a lot of questions that only I could answer, I was told. The inference was that I was spending too much time in the head office or that our advertising promotion was deficient. A lot of pressure was put on me before I finally decided to take the trip. I was told that only I could dissipate the rumors circulating about our financial difficulties, which did not exist at the time. The representatives evidently felt that they were doing all they could and that it was high time they got some help from New York, meaning me. I talked over the trip with Wilton and he agreed with me that the trip might well be instructive and constructive. And on one opportune day I set off.

In Cleveland, which had been the temporary home of Time at one period of its development, I was treated with hostility in some quarters, coolness in others and seldom with any show of interest. Newsweek? Don't know it or never read it. Too much like Time. Why have two news magazines?

Newsweek is not as readable as Time. And so on even to the point of being told that I was butting my head against a stone wall and as an extension of that idea I had better quit while the quitting was good. I do not of course remember any particular conversation in Cleveland. That it was pretty grim and that nobody seemed to be interested in me or Newsweek I still have, when I think of it, a faint disagreeable recollection. Nor do I recall having made the slightest personal impression on those people. Their minds were just closed to me.

I was pretty low in my mind as John Roney, our representative at that time in that part of the country, and I made our way to Akron to see Paul Litchfield, President of the Goodyear Tire and Rubber Company. Mr. Litchfield received me coldly and after listening to me he admitted reluctantly, it seemed, that I might have something at that. But, he added, Newsweek is too new and too small for us, a refrain I was to hear many times before I got back to New York. On leaving Mr. Litchfield promised to read Newsweek, but whether he did or not I never knew as I did not see him again.

My interview with Harvey Firestone was warm and friendly and for the first time I came face to face with a man who preferred Newsweek to Time. He asked a great many questions, I remember, and I left him with the feeling that I had finally accomplished something, even though there did not appear to be any immediate business forthcoming. The Firestone Tire and Rubber Company was strictly from Missouri when it came to advertising appropriations. But John

Roney was not only satisfied but enthusiastic. He knew the
people I had been talking to and I did not. I had answered the
questions that had been worrying him, and he assured me that
I had made a good impression. This was at least a sign that I
had bolstered John's confidence.

In Detroit my reception was memorable personally, if
mixed as far as Newsweek was concerned. My impression today is that most of the top executives in the automobile industry with whom I spoke told me they preferred Newsweek
to Time, principally on the basis that we were more informative, serious and less flippant. This feeling was not repeated,
unfortunately, in the lower executive echelons. This sector of
the industry echoed the same opinions I had heard in Ohio:
too new, too small. I then began to ask how big we had to be
before we could expect our share of automobile advertising.
The consensus for the entire trip was never less than 200,000.
At that level of circulation, I was informed, Newsweek would
be interesting to a large and important section of national advertisers. Our representative Bob Stewart had arranged an extensive program for me. I was to meet Alfred Sloan, but he
was not in Detroit at the time and I never did meet him subsequently, except in the company of hundreds of other men
at the annual Automobile Show in New York, or at the official
cocktail party held in connection with it. But I did meet one
of the Vice Presidents of General Motors whose name now
escapes me as does the tenor of our conversation. The General Motors personality I remember most clearly was a man

named Curtis, then the President of the Buick Division. Mr. Curtis received me sympathetically and asked some thoughtfully penetrating questions. I think he was trying to discover for his own satisfaction how anyone could be so foolhardy as to start a new magazine at what proved to be the bottom of the Great Depression. His interest was focused on how I had and actually was financing the magazine. I told him candidly, particularly stressing how we kept track of our growing reader interest in the magazine and adding that our stockholders were mostly rich men well able to provide whatever funds we might require in the future. This statement was correct at the time and continued to be valid for another two years. My information seemed to interest and satisfy Mr. Curtis who promised to read Newsweek with more care, by which I was given to understand that he had not until that time read it at all.

At 2 o'clock one afternoon during my stay in Detroit Bob Stewart had arranged for an interview with Henry Ford and his able right hand man, William Cameron. I remember the time for it was an important element in my meeting with Mr. Ford. Bob had gone to a great deal of trouble to arrange this meeting and set great store by it. He told me that he did not expect any immediate results from it but that if the interview went off well it would be of great assistance to him. This put me fairly on the spot. The idea was to have a talk with Mr. Cameron first and afterward with Mr. Ford. We arrived punctually and I was immediately presented to Mr. Cameron by

Bob Stewart in a sort of anteroom full of people. Bob had previously told me that Cameron was more important than his boss insofar as advertising went, and I accordingly put myself out to be as agreeable and expansive with him as I possibly could. I found Mr. Cameron easy to talk to but not much interested in hearing about Newsweek from me. He said he knew all about it from Bob Stewart, whom he evidently liked and of whom, I was to discover later, he had a good opinion. He told me that he personally liked Newsweek, and that Mr. Ford read it in preference to Time. He then made me a dissertation on how busy Mr. Ford was with great and important demands on his time. He made no bones about having arranged the interview as a favor to Bob, with the inference that my visit was one of courtesy and not of the least importance to Mr. Ford. He added that the interview was conditioned by Bob's agreement that I would say what I had to say what I had to say to Mr. Ford and leave promptly. And would I please understand that on no account was I to stay more than 10 minutes. I gathered that Mr. Ford loved to talk and that somehow or other I was to shut him up when my time was up and stride out. I could see the reason for all this because around and about were several other people who wanted to see Mr. Ford. But the best laid plans of mice and men.....

It must have been 2:30 p.m. when I was ushered into Mr. Ford's office and introduced to him and it must have been well after 5 o'clock when I left. I distinctly remember that the light was beginning to fail and that it was dark when we got back to Detroit. I was glad that I did not encounter Mr. Cameron as I went out.

My first and only meeting with Mr. Ford was not only the highlight of my trip but a milestone in my life. From the moment that he first looked at me he made me feel at home and I had the feeling that he was prepared to like me, doubtless as a result of my advance publicity via Bob. What I saw before me was one of the most unpretentious men it has even been my good fortune to meet, considering his enormous wealth and power. For me he had a magnetic personality. He spoke to me simply, with great authority on the subjects he was interested in, and appeared to be interested in everything I had to say to him. He had evidently been told that I had been an officer in the British Royal Flying Corps because that knowledge touched off an inquiry into some technical problem in which Mr. Ford was deeply interested. Try as I will I cannot remember the subject the subject of the ensuing discussion. But I do remember Mr. Ford saying to me that he personally could not answer my question but that he had someone who could. He there upon telephoned for his chief engineer to come over from the River Rouge Plant. He did this before I realized what was happening and before I could demonstrate with him, as I felt duty bound to do, with some such remark as please don't bother. I had no chance to say anything and I felt that my reputation must have plunged to an all-time low as far as Mr. Cameron was concerned. While we were waiting for the engineer, Mr. Ford kept up a lively conversation with me about how I happened to found Newsweek, occasionally referring to his experiences in the founding of the Ford Motor Company. He was frequently interrupted on the telephone and I could judge from his end of the conversations that I was playing havoc with his appointments for the afternoon. I did offer to wait in the anteroom until the engineer arrived, but Mr. Ford would have none of it. Mr. Ford did most of the talking and I set spellbound listening to him and answering his questions.

When the engineer finally arrived, the conversation turned into a dialog between them with me on the sidelines listening. My only recollection of the subject discussed is that it was highly technical and way above my understanding. I do recall being very much impressed with Mr. Ford's grasp of the subject and his ability with leading questions that elicited the information he was after. And never once did he leave me out in the cold, explaining various points in simple language for my understanding. It is shameful that I cannot now remember any of it. Hard as I try it remains elusive. Perhaps one day it will pop into my consciousness again.

When the interview finally came to an end Mr. Ford asked me how long I was staying in Detroit, saying that he would like to show me over his River Rouge plant. As I was at the end of my stay I had to thank him and refuse his invitation. If I had then known that I was not to see him again I should most certainly have prolonged my stay. He said I must do it when I came back. He thought I would be very interested and that it was a sight well worth seeing. "Just send me a telegram when you are coming back and I will take a day off and personally conduct you." I thanked him again and drew his attention to my wooden leg, which greatly surprised him, and said that my walking was severely limited, especially on hard surfaces. He told me I would not have to do any walking and that he would take me over the plant in a specially designed factory car. It is one of my keenest disappointments that I never saw him again. I never met Mr. Cameron again either.

Another meeting I enjoyed was with the President of the Packard Motor Company. If my recollection is correct, he also had been born in England. He was a good salesman and tried to get me to buy a Packard. I told him that I could not possibly afford one, but that I would buy one when Newsweek went into the black. He then said that if I would buy a car, he would use the proceeds to advertise in Newsweek. I said I would think about it. I did not take his offer seriously and nothing came of it. All I got out of the meeting was the satisfaction of knowing that he read Newsweek in preference to Time principally because it was less flippant, a common opinion.

The next day off to Chicago and Jack Rutherford, our representative there. My reception was not so good as it had been in Detroit but better than it had been in Cleveland. So far as Newsweek was concerned, most of the people I saw were on the fence waiting to see what happened to us, for the rumors of our impending failure were widespread. I told all such

doubting Thomases that there was not any possibility of failure and why, without feeling that I was believed. Some people
liked Newsweek but always with the reservation, in regard to
advertising, that it was too new, too small. I remember getting
a lot of advice including "why don't you fold it up." The Chi-
cagoans did not pull any punches.

When I got back to New York, I held a series of confer-
ences with Ted Rea and asked him to make a further investigation into the "too new, too small" argument and the
question of a circulation level of 250,000 readers. My recollection is that Ted reported that most advertisers were of the
same opinion. I also told Ted that, based on my observations,
the proper way to sell space in Newsweek was by selling it as
part of the newsmagazine market. Ted had already thought
about that and was doing it, but evidently had not got it over
to his salesman. In developing my thoughts, I said that I
thought advertisers were accustomed to buying their newsmagazine cake in one piece. What we had to do was to educate
them to buy a small part of the same cake, and later on to
buying our whole cake made from the same recipe, which
could not then be reached by buying the much bigger Time
cake. All this was agreed to between us, but still we were far
behind our scheduled volume.

In regard to building up rapidly to 250,000 circulation it
was obviously going to cost a lot more money and rapidly
would mean at least two years before we could achieve such a
program. We had a sound foundation for such growth. Our

conversions from short to long-term subscriptions had increased slightly and our renewals of long-terms were much better than I had estimated, about the only instance in which my anticipations were exceeded. Looking backward I think it was the fact that we had demonstrated for the first time that we had created a place in the market for a second newsmagazine, even though this result might not yet be conclusive on a volume basis, that decided me to recommend the increase. The objective was to secure a greater volume of advertising as soon as possible, which was just what we were lacking. This I now recognize was not a wise decision on my part, as things turned out. The decision itself was sound but it had to be accompanied by a steady supply of money and by a progressive increase in advertising income. One would not come without the other.

In due course I made a report to the Board of Directors on the results of my trip west, which may be summarized for the sake of convenience:

1) That our current information showed that as many people preferred Newsweek to Time as vice versa

2) That most advertisers I had talked with were of the opinion that we were too young and too small to attract national advertising.

3) That a great many advertising men thought we would have to get to a net paid circulation of 250,000 before we would interest big advertisers, which would take time and money.

Wilton Lloyd-Smith and Winky Child were enthusiastic over the report, which was all that mattered. The sense of the Board was that we should concentrate on circulation expansion. How much would it cost? I told them there were too many variables involved to give a quick or accurate estimate. I told them it would take a minimum of two years to reach such a level and that much would depend on what happened in the interim. I said that I was reasonably sure that money invested in circulation would return to us with an eventual profit and that we should be absolutely sure by the following spring. My great worry was advertising. Ted Rea was still able to reassure them on that score. The directors were fully aware that we were running a budgetary deficit that would have to be made good and this would have to be added to the cost of the new program under discussion. Subsequently we held another meeting in Wilton Lloyd-Smith's office in Wall Street, during which Wilton had a hair cut in it. I asked for $250,000 and got it, on the basis of contributions from leading stockholders. I remember that Paul Mellon subscribed $50,000 and I think it was then that Jock Whitney became a stockholder. It was understood that still more money would be required to complete the program, but that was a detail that the directors were not prone to remember.

On one occasion before this when we were scraping the bottom of the barrel, Helen and I were invited by Winky's mother and father to the engagement ball given in honor of their daughter, Barbara. One of my many handicaps is having

Celtic blood in my veins. When Celts are up they are very, very up, and when they are down God help them. And they can go up and down with lightening rapidity. I was in the downs that night, about as down as I get, which is plenty down, a thoroughly impossible mood, until Helen and the champagne pulled me out of my doldrums. But my bad behavior did not escape the perception of old Mr. Childs. A few days later I was summoned to his office in Wall Street and from there taken to lunch at the Bankers Club.

Chapter Seven

Seeds of Doubt

Starling Childs was a magnificent specimen of manhood, well over six feet tall, handsome, well proportioned, erect and vigorous at somewhere near seventy years at that time. As he strode from his office on the wait to the club, I had difficulty keeping up with him. Winky was also present and after the lunch old Mr. Childs wanted to know what was bothering me. Although I was pretty sure he already knew what was bothering me, for I kept nothing from Winky, I told him. His next question convinced me that the meeting had been set up for a definite reason. Didn't I think I was trying to do too much. I told him that that was probably so and that I was plenty tired, but saw no practical way out of it. He asked me if I would welcome assistance, to which I replied that I would. He then told me that a friend of his had connection in the newspaper world and might be able to suggest someone. I said that I would appreciate and welcome the assistance of a good, experienced business manager, but that there was no money available for one and that I was reluctant to ask the directors to take on another relatively high salaried man at this point. I believe that Mr. Childs spoke to Wilton Lloyd-Smith later on and the matter was settled.

And that is how I managed to acquire Jack Bresnahan as the first business manager of Newsweek, one-time business manager of the defunct New York World. Although I welcomed him sincerely, warmly and even enthusiastically, his coming to Newsweek was a major disaster for me. Looking back over the years, with every desire to be just, I am unable to escape judging him responsible for undermining the confidence which the directors had had in me up to that time. Bresnahan was on the other side of 60 years old at that period, blue-eyed, white-haired, ruddy complexioned and as false as they come. Within six months his objective became clear: he wanted to become publisher of Newsweek under the protection of the Childs family. He evidently felt that his experience entitled him to a better position on the magazine than business manager and that my lack of experience disqualified me for the job of publisher. I seem vaguely to remember that in the beginning he wanted to take me under his wing and teach me the ropes, as it were. Like most over ambitious men he overplayed his hand, was discovered and fell into instant disgrace. But not before he had succeeded in sowing the seeds of doubt in my board of directors.

In the incredibly short space of six months or so, he succeeded in dividing the staff against me, or rather trying to. Instead of having less trouble, I had more trouble and it became more and more obvious to me that Jack was defeating the reasons for his appointment. Not only did he attempt to suborn my staff, but he was entirely successful in dividing the board against me, temporarily. For a time he had Wilton Lloyd-Smith and Howell van Gerbig on his side, until he was discovered. Curiously enough it was Wilton who first lost confidence in him and dubbed him as a trouble maker. He never succeeded in influencing Winky Childs who stood by me, as always, an attitude that did not particularly please his father. When my relations first became strained with Bresnahan, I had a good talk to Wilton Lloyd-Smith about what I thought the cause of it all was. To my surprise I got no sympathy for my side of the case. Wilton, in one of his semi-jocular retorts accused me of being jealous of Bresnahan. This enraged me because whatever I felt about Bresnahan, it was not prompted by jealousy.

I no longer remember if Bresnahan became a director. If he did, it was because I wanted him there as a mark of the confidence which the Childs family and I reposed in him. If he was not, he certainly attended more than one meeting of the board. Thus he was fully consulted on policy and in the beginning of his tenure of office not a single step was made without his consent and approval. So long as all went well there was no trouble from him; but when they did not he took refuge in the simple expedient of denying that he had approved the measure in question. This was stupid performance because there were always witnesses to the contrary. When faced with them, he pleaded misinformation and misunderstanding. A case in point was circulation. One of the first things I asked Bresnahan to do was to make an exhaustive examination of our circulation structure and methods. I told him that I knew we were overloaded with short-term subscriptions, but as these were converting satisfactorily I would like him to limit his inquiry to finding out how far we could go along the road we had chosen with safety and a reasonable outlay of capital. He was already aware of and in agreement with the advisability of reaching a paid up circulation of 250,000 as soon as possible; he was to make any recommendation that occurred to him. In due course, the study was completed, examined and agreed upon by all the parties concerned.

Sometime afterward a serious error was discovered in our circulation calculations. I naturally looked to Bresnahan for an explanation. He resented my attitude and pointedly gave me not the least satisfaction. That was the start of the vendetta he instigated against me. The discrepancy in our circulation, while not serious, nevertheless could not be cured by direct mail for various reasons. Against my will and inner convictions, I was forced to extend the operations of our field force which up to that time was restricted to obtaining new sub-

scriptions, that is it was not allowed to secure renewals. Bresnahan wanted to give all renewals back to the field force, that
is to say that expiring or expired subscriptions secured by the
field force were to be given back to the field force as prospects. This meant in practice that we would not receive any
income from this source, and I refused to go along with the
suggestion. My argument was based on the fact that at this
stage of the operation it cost us only a few cents to collect $4
a subscription, an income that we could not afford to give
away to placate the field force. I did agree to let the field force
sell short-term subscriptions, the so-called trial offers, and to
turn over all expirations after they had been circularized once
to the field force. That meant that we would take the cream
off the renewals before they got to the field force, and in this
way would avoid the accusation of forcing circulation. Dave
Rohn, the field force manager, agreed reluctantly to the arrangement and in the end became satisfied with it.

But not Jack Bresnahan. He would agree to nothing. He
denied any responsibility for the error that had made the new
field force arrangement necessary and even went so far as to
say he had ever agreed to an increase in our circulation. In the
bitter argument that followed these denials, it became apparent that Bresnahan did not understand our direct mail operations and had contributed nothing to the study I had ordered,
much less do any work on it. From that time on, Jack and I
were to become deadly enemies. He took his views over my
head to the board of directors. The directors naturally heard

my side of the questions raised by Bresnahan and decided to hold a special meeting to hear both of us. The meeting, and a very stormy one it was, took place in Wilton's apartment on Gracie Square one fine Sunday morning. Bresnahan's principal contribution to the meeting was his oft reiterated remark that what Newsweek needed was a new publisher, with the inference that he was available.

Even if I had been more diplomatic with Bresnahan, I do not think I could have prevented his subsequent downfall. He was a bad actor, inborn, and a pompous egotist. Wilton referred to him as a "truculent cockatoo." He had little native ability and poor judgment. On top of everything else he was a scheming opportunist as ambitious as they come and totally devoid of ethics. I discovered too late that he had a reputation for playing politics on The World. Since Jack remained impenitent I was obliged to force him off the staff.

Old Mr. Childs was of course disappointed, and he came to my office to tell me so in no uncertain language. He had done his best to help me and the inference was that I had acted in a most ungrateful manner. There was little I could say to him. He had acted in good faith and it was certainly not his fault that his nominee, if I can call Bresnahan that, had turned out so badly. And I was far from thinking it was mine. Winky eventually got him to see the episode in a different light. Wilton Lloyd-Smith had been very much impressed with Bresnahan and I think the other directors were, too. That Wilton eventually backed me up was far from being a personal triumph for me. My relations with my board were never to be on the same footing again. Bresnahan had in fact won an important battle.

Chapter Eight

Popularity Contest

Whoever suggested and arranged for me to meet President Roosevelt in the White House I do not recall, nor why it was done. The interview which the President granted me was to have a curious similarity as to subject matter with my first meeting with Wilton Lloyd-Smith and on the time element with my reception by Henry Ford. When I duly arrived at the White House for my appointment, the anteroom outside the President's office was full of people, including Jo Davidson, the sculptor, all waiting to see the Chief Executive. The press secretary was not pleased to see me and had little or no compunction in treating me as very small fry. He told me peremptorily that my audience was limited to five minutes. I asked him who was going to keep track of the time, he or I. He said at the end of five minutes he would enter the President's office as a signal to me to get up, make my excuses and get out. He said that the President loved to talk, but that he had a busy morning ahead of him and I was to cooperate. And I could see that he meant it and I could see the reason why by looking around the anteroom.

Although I was far from being a political follower of President Roosevelt, I was impressed, despite myself, with his impelling personality and captivated by his seductive charm of manner. Within seconds he made me feel at ease almost at home, by his simple informality. He asked me some sharp questions about Newsweek and congratulated me on having the courage to start a new enterprise when I did and a lot of complimentary effusion. Then, without a pause, he switched abruptly to Henry Luce. I don't know what Harry had done to merit this singular abuse, for abuse it was, from the President of the United States, but I thought it was a back-handed compliment. The President was well launched on his philippic against Luce when the secretary entered. I obediently stood up, but was told to sit down and the secretary was dismissed in an intimately friendly manner, only to reappear every few minutes or so with a "Mr. President, I must remind you..." But it was quite useless. The President had no intention of being cheated out of his diatribe against Luce.

What the President had to tell me about Luce was off the record and shall remain so. All I can say is that it was vitriolic and, although I was far from friendly with Luce myself, it embarrassed me. I could not imagine why the President of the United States had chosen me to confide in or what value it had for him. The only thing I could think of was that he knew we were competitors and either assumed or had been informed that we were not on friendly terms, and was trying to make me feel happy in the knowledge that I had an ally. All I can still say is that Luce's offense must have been monstrous so intensive was his vehemence and so deep his feelings against Luce.

In an attempt to end this uncomfortable phase of the interview, I took the first opportunity to ask the President a question. That added several minutes to the interview. My only intention was to get the President out of his obsession with Luce. The President had previously mentioned something about the popularity of his Administration and I asked him how he was sure that it was so. Up to that time, I had had no idea that the Presidency ran a popularity contest on a huge scale. The President told me how it was done in considerable detail, including the measurement of applause or the lack of it in every major movie house in America, whenever the President or a member of his Cabinet appeared on the screen in connection with an important event related to the policy of the Administration. And each movie house was weighted for its snob, upper, middle or popular class frequency. When I was finally able to take my leave of the President, the interview had lasted many times the five minutes scheduled for it. I have no idea how long it was but a very clear recollection of the dirty look I got from the secretary as I left.

When I analyzed the interview I found that all I had gotten out of it, and I was proud to report it, that the Head of the

Nation was a keen Newsweek fan. This news was of course
not surprising. The President told me that he thought we had
a greater respect for the news and that our judgment was better than Time's. He, in common with a great many people, did
not like Time's pertness. Above all he thought we were more
accurate and independent in our editorial treatment of the
news. Sam Williamson was very satisfied when I told him.

After two years of more or less checkered existence
Newsweek was beginning to gather momentum in every department except advertising where we were badly out of kilter
with our estimates. The directors were plainly disturbed and
began putting pressure on me to do something about it. Wilton Lloyd-Smith invited me to dinner to discuss the advertising situation. He did not pull his punches. Ted was a very nice
fellow and all that ,but none of his forecast had come anywhere near realization. It was not the time to say that that was
partly the fault of the directors. Wilton was much too much
disturbed for that. He told me bluntly that it was my responsibility and wanted to know how long I intended to put up
with Ted. I said that Ted was a co-founder of the magazine,
had worked very hard at his job, and I thought we should not
be too precipitate in our decisions. Wilton said we could not
afford any sentiment, that what we were interested in was results. No argument about that. I stalled him with the suggestion that I make a quick visit to our representatives and find
out what they thought of the situation. I added that such a

visit was in any event overdue. Wilton agreed and I set off on my tour.

The reception that I got from our representatives and the advertisers I was able to talk to was very different from the one I had received before. Whereas praise for Newsweek was the exception, this time it was the rule. I will not say that more people liked our magazine than liked Time. My impression was that just as many people liked one as liked the other. Many people told me they preferred Newsweek to Time because of our more conservative treatment of the news. I likened the two news magazines to two newspapers. Some people read the Tribune and others preferred the News. On that parallel I added that one newsmagazine could not be all things to all people. I told them of our fast growing circulation and our fact-finding analyzes of it. I pointed out that we were reaching a sizable executive market, the men who influenced or made buying decisions, high income readers in the professional classes as well as businessmen, and were preferred to Times in some schools and colleges. None of these people could be reached by advertising in Time. I said that the existence and growth of Newsweek was proof that Time did not, and never could reach the entire newsmagazine potential.

I underlined my belief that the efforts of the two news magazines were complementary, jointly enlarging the newsmagazine field and constantly developing a rich market for almost everything with a national distribution. And I emphasized over and over again that Newsweek had captured an important segment of that market and that advertisers would have to advertise in Newsweek to get complete coverage. My remarks seemed to be well received and in many quarters I was promised more consideration in the future. We did not get it, or rather not much more. Why?

I discovered why in my discussions with our representatives. There was almost total agreement with each other in their points of view. All of them said I had made statements that they knew nothing about and of which they should have been well and continuously informed and complained with some asperity that they were not being supported by the head office. This was to some extent a criticism of me and I had to take it. Some of it I could discount because I knew they had received plenty of information about our circulation; analysis had gone out to them as soon as it was available. Evidently it was not reaching them in a form they could make effective use of. I did not let the criticism pass and accused them of not knowing how to make use of the material sent to them. This accusation provoked a different argument from each of them and I no longer remember the details. I recall only two things about the arguments put forward. Both were personal. One concerned Ted, who was criticized for the first time openly, though diplomatically. The other was for me to make more frequent trips to their respective territories. The frequency they wanted would have turned me into an advertising manager and I could deduce from that that Ted was not giving them the support they required nor the information which as a director was in his knowledge. I told them I would make regular trips thereafter but that they could not be as frequent as they wanted because I had other things to do. It was also plain that we were not paying enough attention, which also meant we were not spending enough money, on advertising promotion. Something drastic had to be done.

When I got back to New York I discussed my findings with Wilton Lloyd-Smith before presenting a report to the board. Since I knew beforehand that Wilton would ask me what my conclusion was about Ted I felt obliged to voice the criticisms I had heard of him. He asked me if I had anyone in mind to replace him. I said I would talk to someone, see if he were interested, and report back. I was very unhappy about this development, but I had to admit that Ted, with the best of intentions, had misled us throughout 1934 in respect to advertising, insisting on the validity of his rate holders. Even in the latter part of the year he still insisted that they would be converted into orders. While all this was undoubtedly so, another element had to be considered: the responsibility of the directors for our financial instability, which made Ted's job a very difficult one. It was impossible for me to insist on this point in view of the fact that I was about to ask for another large amount of money. As I look back on it I do not even now think that there was anything I could have done to have saved Ted.

It so happened that Mary Hincks, whom I had known ever since I arrived in the United States, had married Florimond

DuSossoit (who afterward changed his name to F. DuSossoit Duke) had invited Helen and me to dinner in their new $100,000 house in Connecticut. At that time Duke was advertising director of Fortune. During one of our conversations Mary delivered herself of a feminine outburst against Harry Luce for reasons I no longer recall. It seemed that the dislike of Luce was becoming a national pastime. Although Duke said nothing, I gathered from Mary that he was dissatisfied with his current job on the argument that he had got about as far as he was likely to get in the Time organization.

With this dinner party in mind and Mary's fulminations, I had lunch with Duke, who had been a good friend of mine since before his marriage to Mary. I told him Ted had resigned, which was not strictly true, and that I was looking for an experienced advertising manager. I made it clear that I did not want an advertising salesman but a man who had had actual experience as and success in the position of advertising manager. Since I was sure he knew several people in such a position could he recommend somebody? Or at the very least, point someone out to me. Duke said the obvious, that he would have to think about it. I figured he would discuss it with Mary and that if he should be interested himself he would have to come to me. He was interested and he came to me. We did not discuss terms and conditions at that time because I wanted to be sure of my authorization before doing so.

When I got back to Wilton Lloyd-Smith I told him I had a man in mind and went on to tell him about Duke. I said that he was a good friend of mine some eight years standing and had been an usher at my wedding with Helen. I told him that Duke had been a space salesman for Time and had worked his way up to his present position as advertising director of Fortune. I said that Duke was interested in principle and that I wanted authorization from the board to deal with him. By the time I got through, Wilton was impressed and wanted to know what we would have to pay a fellow like Duke. I said that I guessed that he must be getting $25,000 a year and that we would have to pay him more than that in order to get him to leave Fortune or that much and an interest in the business, plus a vice presidency and a directorship. I said I would take care of the stock interest if the board approved the rest. I stressed the point that it would be a great thing for Newsweek if we could get a man of Duke's caliber, but that it would be a waste of time and money to get him if our recurrent financial crises were to continue, that no matter how good Duke might be he would be powerless in respect to new advertising business unless we were adequately financed through a new capitalization and calls upon money as we needed it. Wilton was getting used to this argument and I thought he regarded it as one of my stratagems to get more money. He reminded me that I had made a lot of estimates and budgets and that none of them was any good. I said true enough but that the board, which had been kept well informed, knew why they were no good. Then he logically wanted to know how much more money we were going to need before we reached the break-

even point. I told him that only God knew. We were committed to a circulation program that would continue to cost
money for perhaps another two years or so and that I could
give him as an approximation of what that would cost. The
rest would depend on how many pages of advertising we were
able to sell and that depended to a major extent on having the
ready capital. Then he wanted to know where all the money
had gone to and was clearly getting impatient with me. I reminded him that he had said on several different occasions
that Newsweek was a valuable property. The money had gone
into making it a valuable property, but that it would not continue to become a valuable property unless it was properly
supported. He replied that there seemed to be no end to it. I
said that the drain on capital would surely end when we began
to sell from 15 to 20 pages of advertising per issue. Then he
wanted to know about circulation and it occurred to me that
he had confused the profit I had talked about as meaning a
profit for the entire operation. I told him that circulation
would eventually pay for itself but that the income above that
point would never, by the greatest stretch of the imagination,
pay for the editorial department and the costs of production
and distribution. He seemed surprised. I told him that it was
not the first time I was telling him this. At this point we had
spent close to $750,000 and he wanted to know if another
$250,000 to $300,000 was put in if that would do the trick. I
told him again that I did not know and could not tell. Everything depended on advertising income and that we could not

expect miracles from Duke right away. I thought it would be at least six months before he began to produce. He then said something about having a bear by the tail.

We then went back to Duke and he told me to go ahead and make him the offer I had in mind subject to the approval of the board and that he would meantime sound them out. He thought that the better way of handling the matter rather than going to them twice. I knew that if Wilton was in favor of the change the other directors would follow along. I said not to forget that it was not only a question of $25,000 for Duke but that he might want a bigger budget for his department. I fore-stalled him from asking how much by saying that we would probably know how much only after Duke had started to work for us. He then startled me by saying that it was also a question of raising my salary to $25,000. He said he did not consider it would be practical politics for me to be receiving less than Duke. I thanked him and said that that would not be necessary and that I would not accept it. I also told him that he should have a talk with Ted. This he promised to do.

I have reconstructed the above conversation with Wilton Lloyd-Smith as having taken place in a single meeting purely as a measure of convenience. All the statements made therein were probably spoken on several different occasions. And I have reconstructed it in such detail because of its importance in the events that followed. Naturally I no longer remember in every instance the actual language employed. I remember the sense of each point in discussion and that such points were covered at one time or another.

My first step after leaving Wilton was to talk to Ted. It was a painful business for both of us, I guess. I wanted desperately to find some other position for him, but with Newsweek operating at a loss, it was out of the question. Ted took it well, at least on the surface, and resigned. I was now free to talk with Duke. I made him that offer I had outlined to Wilton and he accepted, subject to my assurances that he would be loyally supported by the directors with the necessary capital in order to make it possible for him to work. I reminded him that he was soon to become a director and would have a voice and vote in its deliberations.

The meeting of the Board of Directors that approved the deal I had made with Duke was a memorable one for a good many reasons. First, for its enthusiasm. Everyone was pleased with Duke's appointment and, like a lot of little boys, expected miracles from him. I remember that I came in for praise for having induced Duke to come in with us, which was a miracle in itself. Second, the meeting was notable for its obfuscation over the matter of money. It was perfectly obvious that Duke's salary would raise the budget that much more, plus additional expenses; but when I asked for that much more than I had previously been talking about I had a rough time of it. I was accused of always asking for more money in an atmosphere of annoyance. It was Wilton who once more came to my rescue with the statement that he was convinced we had a valuable property and that it was worth saving. While I was grateful for the first part of his statement, I was mad at the second. There was no question of saving Newsweek. It was a matter of financing it adequately and not piecemeal and I said so. This was thrown back in my face by the allegation that I never could tell them how much I wanted. And I had to go all over this point again. In the end it was agreed that Winky and I would once more approach his father. Wilton and Howell van Gerbig promised $25,000 each. I was to talk to some other stockholders and Wilton said he would talk with E. Roland (Bunny) Harriman and Marshall Field.

At the lunch which followed the meeting, which was again held in Wilton's office, Wilton voiced the opinion that I was a good promoter, the inference being that I was not a good administrator. This remark offended me, which it probably should not have done, because I felt it was unjust. Every single director present was in agreement with Wilton that Newsweek was a very valuable property, as he had expressed it. Who had made it a valuable property, I asked? On the stockholder's money was the retort. This jibe incensed me and I asked if that was not always the case with any enterprise, particularly a new one. They agreed that that was so, but added that Newsweek was using up too much money. Look at what Time has done with only $87,000. Since we had covered this point more than once it was obvious that the remark had been made out of annoyance with me. It did give the opportunity for plain speaking and I said that one of the reasons it was costing so much was the lack of advertising revenue and the absence of a well-defined financial policy, which was also their responsibility. I added that if Newsweek were the valuable property they said and believed it was, it was surely worthwhile to support it by revamping the entire capital structure in order to give us a reasonable reserve of cash or dependable calls on cash. Finally, in a conciliatory mood, they admitted that our main worry was lack of advertising income and that with the advent of Duke things should go better. Provided that there are no more financial crises, I added.

The financial results of this meeting, while it produced all the money I had asked for eventually, it came irregularly in relatively small amounts, despite the schedule I made for the actual payments. There was not the slightest possibility of getting it all at once. And, if we had to go along in this way, it did not matter so long as the payments were made on their scheduled dates, which they were not, and because of it we were to have one or two more financial crises. All my warnings, pleas and expositions were so many words, unheeded at that. Obviously we could not go on in this way. It was unfair to the "property" and in actual fact a breach of contract with Duke. I got $50,000 from the Childs, and $25,000 from Wilton promptly. Wilton arranged for me to see Bunny Harriman who wanted to see me before making a decision. It took time. Eventually I had an appointment to meet him in his Fifth Avenue house early one evening, but when I got there he was going out with his daughters to a party. We shook hands, exchanged some pleasantries, and we both left in opposite directions. As far as I recollect I never saw or talked with Mr. Harriman again. But I got his check for $25,000 a little later on. Wilton must have done a good job on him. He was however unable to interest Marshall Field who was probably full of his own publishing problems at the time. Howell van Gerbig had to get his money from his family and he was always late in carrying out his engagements.

The following incident is related only to show the degree of irresponsibility I had to put up with. Van arrived at my office one morning, conversed amiably and animatedly with me for a few minutes, put a check face down on my desk just out of my reach and abruptly left. When I picked up the check it was for $15,000 instead off the $25,000 he had promised. Since the payment was made weeks late and we needed the money, the Childs had to make the deficiency good.

What I did not know at this time, neither did Winky Childs, was that the directors began to meet in secret, that is, behind our backs. The reason for the exclusion of Wink was undoubtedly that they knew he would tell me of their conclaves. The objective of these meetings was to take care of any future monetary requirements. I do not think these meetings were aimed against me personally, or at least not in the beginning, because in the end I was told about them. That they were fed up with me I do not deny and to a certain extent I can sympathize with them. Why they did not take me into their confidence, I still cannot figure out, unless they felt I was planning a similar move. It was not the case, but I should have been.

On a move made by Ward Cheney, Frank White was appointed as business manager with my full acquiescence. Before coming to us, Frank had worked for a man named Ginsberg, a friend of Ward's, in the book publishing business. Frank was an expert accountant, friendly and helpful, and I liked him personally, but could never get over the feeling that he was Ward's man. Neither by word nor action did he ever give me cause to suspect; but I have often wondered, and I still do, what part he played behind the scenes in the events to come, if indeed he played any part. Perhaps all this is pure imagination on my part. Under the circumstances that existed at the time, his job with us was not much of a challenge to him and I do not think it would have been for many years to come when Newsweek would be forging ahead. He subsequently became the Treasurer of Weekly Publications Inc. under Vincent Astor, but he did not stay in that position very long. It was with great pleasure that I learned later on that he had been offered and had accepted a position of responsibility with the Columbia Broadcasting Company, subsequently becoming a director, if my information is correct. It was obviously a much bigger opportunity for him.

Chapter Nine

Vincent Astor and Today

At the time of which I am writing I had been in harness, working seven days a week, with very few breaks, for almost three years, two of which were years of strain and harassment. My job was an exacting one at best, but coupled with all the uncertainties and worries over money, it evidently began to affect my health. First Helen got after me to let up and then Wilton Lloyd-Smith, but perhaps for occult reasons of his own. If I had not been so tired and discouraged, I should have probably done what I ought to have done. This was less apparent at the time.

On the one hand I was always able to get what money I needed, after fighting for it, but never when I wanted it. The process was exhausting. It was one thing to get a few tons of thousands here and there, but quite another to go after a few hundred thousand dollars. I know that I should never get the kind of money I was then thinking of from my present directors and probably not through them. The point was that I was thinking about the future and the necessity for adequate capital. So were three of my directors. And one of them about my "health," which was to play a part in the events to come.

The first intimation that my directors were acting independently, although I was too blind to see it at the time, was contained in a visit from Ward Cheney, new obviously at the instigation of Wilton Lloyd-Smith and Howell van Gerbig. Ward was the only son of the eldest son of Colonel Frank Cheney who, although not the founder of that once famous silk empire established under the name of Cheney Brothers, was its mainspring for many years. Ward's father, Charles Cheney, inherited the imperial toga and with it some very imperial ideas. He dominated his brothers and was without doubt one of the most self-important and overbearing men I have ever met. He planned to make Cheney Brothers the General Motors of the silk industry, according to reliable report circulating in the family, but neglected to take even the most elementary precautions to protect the huge raw silk inventory the firm used to carry. When the 1929 crash came, the company lost millions of dollars when the price of raw silk dropped precipitately. And thus Charles' Napoleonic vision evaporated.

When Charles died, the Presidency of the firm went to Ward Cheney instead of one of the surviving brothers, for reasons that are very difficult to understand. His appointment, which must have been approved by his uncles and other relatives, was nevertheless acidly criticized by the younger members of the family. In fairness to Ward it must be said that Cheney Brothers was in a bad way when he took over as its chief executive officer.

The job of putting Cheney Brothers back on its feet was no doubt a tremendous job and a challenging one for a young man of energy and ability. Ward did not have what it took, as the record shows. The affairs of the company went from bad to worse until finally it all but disappeared. Ward's contribution was to preside over its demise. As someone has said, the decline and fall of Cheney Brothers was accentuated by Ward's ineptitude. The most damning disapproval of him was the stricture of being a second-class man with a third-class mind. I have no opinion about this. I found him personally a very pleasant fellow. Before I had got him to become a stockholder and a director of Newsweek, I had known him slightly. He doubtless had a good part of his father's vanity, considerable charm, but evidently nothing of his father's authority. As I got to know him, I was forced to recognize in him a dedicated sycophant of the monied crowd, partly from his known friends and partly from the way he talked about them. He had also married money, which was perhaps the root of his attitudes. He was also a fashionable liberal particularly in the millionaire class, such as Averell Harriman, with whom he had many traits in common. But I liked him, got along with him, and trusted him, despite Helen's oft pronounced warnings. And I was enough attracted to him to ignore Helen's opinion of him on the ground that she was prejudiced and I do not even remember why she detested him so fiercely.

This was the man who came to see me in my office one morning, seeking information about our direct mail procedure. He told me that a friend of his in book publishing business, probably the Ginsburg from whom he had inherited Frank White, was very much interested and would I very kindly tell him about it. I told him about it in more than a little detail in response to his promptings. I only remember one phase of this meeting. I had used as an example a mailing that cost $25,000. I had explained how we tested it and mailed it out in sections to protect ourselves against a drop in our anticipated return. When I told him that each such mailing resulted in an initial loss, Ward thought it was a very risky way of getting subscriptions. He seemed to think that direct mail was an immediate money making proposition. Feeling that he was thinking about the book publishing business, I told him that I had no idea of how direct mail would work out for the sale of books, and added that the risk would possibly not be any greater since there was a risk in putting an advertisement in a newspaper or periodical, a common way of selling books. It might work out and it might not. This did not seem to penetrate Ward's mind. He could not get it out of his mind that we gambled (and that was the word he used) money without knowing what we would get out of it. I repeated that this was not true, that we tested first to find out if the list we proposed to use was any good. I said that there were certain lists that always worked out for us, but even so we always tested them before we used them again. I told him that economic and social conditions often affected even a good list and added by way of example that we had been caught with a small mailing during the week of the moratorium which gave us a poor result. But Ward evidently could not get away from the idea that I had been gambling with the stockholders money. I remember distinctly telling him that Time got its subscriptions pretty much in this way and that if he would talk to Roy Larsen I was sure he would get confirmatory information.

I was not prepared for the sequel and I was in fact not to know of it for some years to come. Ward had been sent by Wilton Lloyd-Smith, and not at all by his book publishing friend, to check up on me through an evaluation of my direct mail methods from the point of view of a business man. Evidently Wilton must have been harboring a suspicion that my methods were not sound and that I was therefore wasting money on them. This idea must have been put into his head during the Bresnahan fracas. At any rate Ward Cheney reported back to Wilton that he (Ward) was convinced that I did not know what I was talking about!

Around this time a remark of Roy Larsen's was reported to me. I do not know whether it was true, but I have always liked to think it was: "Tommy would be okay if his directors would leave him alone."

The directors did not and would not leave me alone. And at the next meeting of the board I found out what they had been up to behind my back. Someone suggested, and I am reasonably sure it was Ward Cheney, that Vincent Astor was about to discontinue the publication of his magazine Today and that there was a possibility of a merger of the two magazines. What did I think of it? What, indeed! I was just too staggered to think clearly. My first reaction was that it was plain idiocy even to contemplate the marriage of Newsweek to a failure. My second thoughts were more reassuring, provided that Newsweek was to absorb Today and not vice avers and that the merger would mean a solution of our financial problems. I was assured that that would surely be the case or no merger. I did not know a great deal about Today. The knowledge that it was not flourishing was as common and widespread as our money troubles were in the marketplace of our business relationships.

I told the directors, when I had recovered from the initial shock, that I was under the impression that Today's circulation would be an expense to us, in fact quite a heavy burden, and that we could not expect much compensation in the way of eventual subscriptions, and for these reasons Today's subscription list could not be taken into account as a positive factor in a merger. I pointed out that the suggested merger would only make sense if Astor were willing to come in on a substantial basis with our own stockholders in a new corporate set-up. Eventually the deal was put up to Astor on that basis and accepted by him.

When I got back to my office, I set to work investigating Today. It was about the same age as Newsweek and had been started by Vincent Astor and Averell Harriman to help Roosevelt popularize the New Deal. It suffered from the same dearth of advertising as Newsweek, but its circulation had never risen above the 75,000 mark. I have forgotten what its newsstand sales were, but they must have been insignificant. A large part of its subscriptions had been sold at cut rates in combination with other magazines, premiums or forced sales. I was correct in my previous estimate that Today's circulation would be practically valueless to us. I was informed that Astor and his henchman Harriman had dropped $3,000,000 on Today, which may have been an exaggeration and I thought it was. Whatever it was, the only way they could get it back was by way of a merger.

The prospect of the merger, despite its possible good points, was very upsetting to me. One of the things that bothered me was the terms upon which a merger could be effected. On the assumption that we formed a new company, I figured that it would cost that company something like $250,000 to fulfill the obvious terms of the merger, i.e. the fulfillment of Today's subscriptions and the cost of transfer to our books, and much more than that if we were obliged to take on any of Today's personnel. Therefore if our stockholders and Astor and Harriman put up equal amounts of cash, which was the way I was thinking of the merger, our stockholders would have to pay half the cost of saving Astor's and Harriman's money, without any practical benefit to them.

It seemed to me therefore that Astor and Harriman should pay a substantial premium for a half share in the new company. It would be different, of course, if our stockholders had no alternative and it was my conviction that they had. There certainly was no reason in the world why our stockholders should pay a premium for the privilege of bailing out Astor and Harriman. The alternative was to go ahead without Today. They had the money and I believed firmly that they would go along in a new capitalization of Newsweek Inc., if a rational and adequate plan had been presented to them.

My objection to the merger was that it was unnecessary. What we needed was more capital and included in it ample reserves to carry us until our advertising sales would carry us and our circulation promotion had ceased to be a burden. The only aspect of the suggested merger that interested me was in having Vincent Astor as a stockholder as distinct from the proprietor of Today. I talked all these thoughts over with Wilton Lloyd-Smith. He thought we never should get Astor to scrap Today to become a simple or even a majority stockholder in Newsweek. He was of the opinion that we should have to offer Astor some face-saving palliative even to induce him to merge. When I brought up the unfair burden that the merger would lay on our own stockholders, he countered by saying that in his opinion the present stockholder would be required to put up less in a merger than they would have to provide without it, judging from past experience. No question that Wilton was thinking of his own position. I thought it would be very much more and told him so, but it was useless. The old confidence was gone.

In the end I had to agree that a merger was the only way in which we could get Astor interested in Newsweek. I thought it was putting the cart before the horse, but I had to go along. Since I had allowed myself to become emotionally involved in those discussions, which was to be my principal weakness in the days to come, Wilton asked me to leave the negotiations in his hands. He said I would be no good at it, holding the views I did. In fact he thought I might spoil them. I told him to go ahead with the negotiations with Astor subject to my approval of the details.

Although I could see the possibility of working out a satisfactory deal with Astor, there was not any certainty about it, and I began to worry about what would happen to us if the merger fell through. It was not a question of losing control of Newsweek. I long ago became resigned to that and to know that it was a certainty whichever way the wind blew. My emotional concern with what was happening together with my sense of responsibility to Newsweek, its readers, its staff, suppliers and stockholders were all separate burdens for me to carry. In reality they did not exist as yet; it was the possibility that they might that was worrying me. It was beginning to be a nightmare for me.

I confided my fears in Winky but he thought I was trying to make a mountain out of a molehill. Perhaps I was, but evidently I was beginning to show it, for the next time I saw Wilton he told me that I was looking like hell, as he expressed it, and I had better go away, a long way away, where I could get an undisturbed rest. There was not much I could do anyway until the negotiations with Astor had been concluded one way or the other. I told him I would think about it. When I told Helen about this conversation, she was one hundred percent in favor of a vacation for me. What she meant was for me to go off alone. I told her that that would be no vacation at all for me, because I would probably start worrying at long range about the whole situation if I did not have her to keep me company and to distract my thoughts from the business. More than that I should probably start worrying about her and the children on top of everything else. Our daughter Laura had been born on Thanksgiving Day of 1935 so that it must have been early in 1936 that this conversation took place. When we came right down to it, we would have to take Laura and nurse, son Howie and ourselves. The expense of such a trip, especially to Bermuda, which we had thought of, put it out of my mind.

It must have been a few days later that Wilton called me up to tell me that the negotiations with Astor were going well and that Astor wanted his man, Gene Forker, the publisher of Today, to be joint publisher with me of Newsweek. Don't say anything now, he added, see him and let me know afterward how you feel about the idea. He then asked me what I had done about a vacation. I said I had discussed it with Helen and that she was in favor of it, but that it was not financially possible at the time. He said that my health was just as important to Newsweek as the merger and that the magazine should pay for it. I refused to consider it at first, but later on, with pressure from Helen, I reconsidered. It so happened that Newsweek, for once in its existence, had a reasonable amount of money in the bank, and I financed the trip by charging it to my expense account to which I had been accustomed to charge my personal expenses when there was not enough money to pay my salary. Astor's financial hounds tried to debit me with the amount of this account later on.

I do not remember how it came about that we went to the Mid Ocean Club in Bermuda but there we went, with Laura, Howie, nurse, maid, Helen and myself. I rented a cottage belonging to the Club at a price far below what we would have had to pay in a hotel and more or less the same as in a pension. Anyway, in my last talk with Wilton I had already stipulated that my salary, which I was given to understand was less than half that of Forker, should be the equal of his if the merger went through. I had no qualms about taking on the extra obligation of the expenses involved, in the event that my accumulated unpaid salary did not cover the debit balance in my expense account.

My meeting with Gene Forker was cordial. Gene was as pleasant to me as flattery would permit. He told me that my conduct of the affairs of Newsweek was nothing short of brilliant. He was full of enthusiasm for the merger and told me he was looking forward to working with me. He also told me that Mr. Astor was looking forward to a meeting with me and a lot about his difficulties with Today. I thought that Gene was probably a heavy drinker, he had the florid complexion of a man who did, but I liked him well enough for a first meeting. I told him that I thought it would be eventually necessary for us to agree on a sphere of action that would limit our respective functions, in order that we could present a united front to the new board of directors. He agreed. I asked him what would interest him most in the new set-up. He said advertising. I said he would have to clear that with Duke and so long as there was no direct interference with him I thought there would be no great difficulty. I then informed him that I was going off to Bermuda - the next day I think it was - and that before I left, I would give orders for him to receive all the information he required and that he was to consider Newsweek his house, or words to that effect. Gene seemed to be very satisfied and pleased, thanked me, wished me a pleasant vacation which he was sure was well earned, and asked my "permission" to send his car to take me to the boat. The meeting broke up on the theme that together we were going to do great things in Newsweek. Nothing could have appeared more auspicious.

Before I left for Bermuda I telephoned Wilton to give him my impressions of Gene Forker and what had transpired at our meeting. I said that I was prepared to accept the designation of joint publisher subject to a definitive agreement regulating our respective functions, something that I thought we could work out between us. Wilton appeared relieved and happy. I left my office in Gene's luxurious automobile in the firm belief that Newsweek's and my own future were secure. I was half right.

In view of what was about to happen in the immediate future I have often wondered, and still do, if my vacation had not been suggested and insisted upon to get rid of me. I did not think of this at the time, but afterward I thought it strange that Vincent Astor had made no move to get in touch with me. I also discovered that Winky Childs, who represented the major stockholding group, had not met him either. And although I had no feeling of insecurity, I do remember clearly being conscious of leaving someone behind me who could be counted on to protest my interests if that became necessary.

Chapter Ten

A Brief Respite

All my life I have been grateful for the respite in Bermuda. I not only remember it, I treasure it, every day of it, more than anything else because it was for the first time that I got to know my four-year-old son Howie and find out for myself what lay behind the face and the voice I was accustomed to see and to hear.

The cottage we had rented from the Mid Ocean Club (of which I subsequently became a member as a token of my confidence in the future) was a dream, just big enough for us all, a bit on the dark side, but supremely comfortable. At the back was a large verandah with a view over our own small dazzling lagoon which in sunlight was pure and brilliant azure. A flower bordered path led from the verandah, past a small aquarium full of bright hued tropical fish, down to a small jetty on the edge of the lagoon. Every day we bathed off the jetty in sparkling seawater. It was ideal for me because I could take off my wooden leg and jump straight into the water and get back again with very little effort up the ladder at the side of the pier. Since I was a devoted fisherman, I immediately set about hiring a small sailboat complete with captain. This was strictly for Howie and me, and we had a barrel of fun out of it.

The cottage was completely set up for housekeeping, or we could have our meals at the club, less than five minutes' walk away. Helen decided that we would be more comfortable, more independent, and have a lot more fun if we had our meals together in the cottage. As I wanted her to be free to play golf with me and to drive around the island to visit nostalgically the places and people we had known on our honeymoon, Helen hired a cook, a very chatty Negro woman, who was exceptionally good and honest to boot. Helen thought also that even with the high price on food on the island plus the cook's wages we would be ahead of the game over the still higher expense of feeding at the Club, not to mention the inconvenience involved, especially on rainy days. And I guess she was right.

In due course the Club arranged the sailboat and captain for us. He was supposed to come and see me the following morning so that I could confirm the deal and find out where we were supposed to pick him up and communicate with him whenever we wanted to go sailing or fishing. We waited and we waited and after a while became aware that someone was yelling at us from behind the cottage. When I went back to the verandah there was the captain on the jetty with a skiff tied to it. Away the other side of our lagoon I could see the mast of the sailboat which the captain had anchored in the Castle Harbor sound. Full of happiness, Howie and I piled into the skiff and were rowed over to the sailboat, about eighteen feet long, mainsail and jib.

The entrance from our lagoon to the Castle Harbor sound was a coral-studded outlet not more than a dozen feet wide. Even the skiff had to be careful picking its way through to the sound. On this particular sunny morning the sound looked like a sun spangled lake, calm and placid, but just below the surface was a vast coral formation. Navigation was limited to a broad canal blasted more or less through the center of it. To reach this canal we had to pass through a smaller canal at right angles to the main one. The outlet to the sea was a mile or more away to the northeast. As the prevailing wind was from the starboard stern quadrant we were soon on the high sea, much to Howie's delight. Papa then took over and under instructions from the captain we made our way, as we did several times afterward, to the extreme north of the islands, anchoring off St. Catherine's Point.

The captain at my request came equipped with a water glass, fashioned out of a small wooden box into the bottom of which was fitted a pane of glass. It was a very efficient little instrument, crude though it was. We soon discovered, however, that we needed two of them, for once Howie had looked through it once he became so excited at what he saw that it was only with great difficulty that I could pry him loose from it long enough to be able to answer the stream of questions he was directing at me.

On that first day, the sea was exceptionally calm and we could keep the water glass on the surface with little difficulty. It was impossible to see the bottom with the naked eye, but once the glass was on the surface a whole new world was opened to us. We could see the bottom between ten and twenty fathoms below us in the minutest detail. Howie was fascinated. Up to that moment his interest had been focused on the tiny aquarium at the cottage. One look at the bottom of the sea and his interest in the aquarium died instantly and totally. I don't think he ever stopped at it again on his way up and down to the jetty.

Far down below the surface were simply thousands of fish, not a few dozen, of such a gay variety of hue and size that were unimaginable for him. There were in plain sight the huge light green morays, tiny little sergeant-majors in black and white stripes, vicious barracuda, groupers, red rock fish, sand sharks, the smaller dark green morays with their yellow markings, and many others of which I too had never seen much less knew their names. The colors were myriad and often startling. There were the red rock fish, blue fish of various shades, bright yellow fish, many different kinds of green fish, fish of every kind of color combination conceivable. And all kinds of strange plant life, some of it too highly colored. All so plainly visible that it seemed we were looking through a giant magnifying glass.

Howie had his curiosity fully aroused and when he saw some bigger fish dart out and eat a smaller one his excitement made me feel that it was worth the whole cost of the trip to see him so utterly happy. And the questions! Look at this. Look at that. What is that? What's the name of that fish? Since he was glued to the water glass we had no way of answering his questions and it was with the greatest reluctance that he would part with it long enough for either the captain or me to get a peep at what he was looking at.

When we later on got the second glass, he soon discovered that I could not answer half of his questions anyway, and from that moment on he attached himself to the captain with whom he became a fast friend, depending on him alone for his information about things marine. He was having such a good time that we tarried over long on our first cruise and arrived back at the cottage very late for lunch, much to Helen's worried annoyance; but when she saw the seraphic glow on Howie's face, she melted instantly.

We made many trips on our sailboat, mostly to the same place to watch the fish through our water glasses, and some-times to other places to fish. If Howie had had his way, he would have gone out every day and stayed out all day. One day we nearly did. We were out a couple of miles fishing when the captain smelled a storm. We hastily put about and ran for the coast and the entrance to the sound, barely getting there before the storm broke. He had furled the mainsail in the nick of time as the gale and the rain hit us. We were wet through in seconds. The rain did not last long but the wind did, and to get back to our lagoon we had to tack from one side of the Castle Harbor canal to the other. Hardly had we got on one tack and we had to put over on the next one. It was frantic exciting work, with Papa at the tiller and the captain prone on the prow signaling me when to come about on the next tack. In the midst of all this, Helen appeared, drenched and alarmed. She had walked around the western shore of the sound near the northern entrance to the channel. At one point she was hardly more than ten yards away from us. She could hear us but we could not hear us her. But she was able to make it plain that she wanted us to hand Howie over to her, though how we were to do that without beaching the boat, I am sure I don't know. She watched us for a while until she evidently felt that we were doing all right, when she went back to the cottage to wait for us. We arrived there none the worse for our experience, just before dark. Helen was distraught and "provoked" but much too glad to see us to get mad at us.

Howie and I went out many times with his new friend the captain. I don't think that Helen ever went with us. I seem to remember that she did not trust the captain's seamanship. She certainly did not trust mine. We found excellent fishing in the channel itself and off the coast of St. David's Island. Once Howie, who was just as keen a fisherman as I, pulled up a dark green moray with a comical look of astonished repugnance on his face. I cut his line and the moray made off with the hook in his mouth. The captain tied a new hook to his line, baited it and threw it out for him. In no time he caught a moray, the same one with the hook still in its mouth for identification. This time the captain kept it and later skinned and filleted it. I must say the snow white fillets looked very appetizing, but I did not dare to take them home to Helen. Most times we took back a good catch off edible fish, often enough to give away to our friends.

One evening, when the cook was off duty, we went to the Club for a few drinks and dinner. It must have been soon after our arrival because we knew none of the members and guests at that time. When we got there, a party of people were having a gay old time for themselves. Helen was immediately spirited away and someone put a drink in my hands, by way of consolation I suppose. Before I could down it, Helen rejoined me and said: "Know what we've done? We've crashed a party." I thought the best thing we could do was to quietly fade away and apologize to our involuntary hosts the next day. Before we could get started, a lady who must have weighed a good two hundred pounds introduced herself by some such fantastic nickname as "Bubbles" Weir, and asked us if we were having a good time. We explained our situation and asked her if she would be kind enough to point out the host and hostess. She said she was the hostess and added playfully that she was not in need of any pointing out. She stood out, she said.

She was, as we discovered then and later, a most delightful person. She told us that she would be very offended if we even thought of leaving and immediately called someone to escort us and introduce us to the others. It turned out that the club had been taken over for that evening by the Weirs of Weirton Steel. They had a house - better call it a palace - just above our cottage. We became good friends for the rest of our visit.

Aside from our sailing, we spent most of our time lazily bathing and golfing. We met a number of people in the Club, had cocktails and meals with them and they with us. We went once over to the other side of the island to visit Mr. Rowley only to find out that he had died a year or so previously. And we went into Hamilton several times on shopping trips which included the purchase of a case of whisky for each adult member of our party, which was then allowed into the States duty free.

Freed from my grinding worries over Newsweek, I soon recovered my spirits and my health. It would be too much to say that I did not ponder the events that had taken place some 800 miles away in New York, nor wonder what was happening there at the time. I did and often. But I had given up worrying about them in which I was profoundly helped by Helen. More than that I felt a certain amount of relief in the hope that what I believed was the last crisis had passed. And at the end of the vacation I was eager to get back and to work under the new regime. And of course I wondered how Gene was getting along. We did not receive any letters, because I had left instructions that none was to be sent. No news is good news!

The time for our departure came all too soon for Howie, who was desolate at having to leave his captain. And we were all a bit sad at leaving our cottage, all except Laura who hadn't a care in the world and was a little butter ball. We promised ourselves that we would return to the same cottage. And so to Hamilton to board the liner that was to take us to New York.

Aboard ship was Leila Luce and her sons, soon to be told that Harry wanted a divorce in order to marry Clare Boothe Brokaw. I saw Harry on the dock in New York from the ship and it was reported to me that he asked for the divorce then and there. If Leila had any glimmerings about the split up, she did not divulge them to Helen. We both felt very sorry for Leila when we heard the news.

Chapter Eleven

The Merger

Before recounting the situation I was to step into at the office and the events that were to follow, it is essential for me to set down the general condition in which Newsweek found itself at that time, and to examine in some detail the position in which I found myself. In doing so, I offer no apology, none is intended, and none is necessary.

In the Fall of 1936, Newsweek's circulation stood at an all-time high of 250,000. This was the figure that I had been competently advised would be an interesting unit for national advertisers, a figure I had recommended to the directors on that basis, and a figure which they had duly authorized. While the original cost of obtaining subscriptions had been much higher than we had estimated, later costs were known to us and our estimates were based on them and thus were realistic. Time's circulation at that point was [not supplied], a figure reached over a period of almost fourteen years, whereas ours had grown to the above volume in a little less than four years.

The inference is implicit that we had grown too fast, and if the surrounding factors are not taken into consideration, it is a valid criticism. As a result of this fast growth our circulation structure was top heavy with short-term subscriptions, every one of which had cost us money. But this was the price we had to pay for reaching the not inconsiderable circulation of 250,000 in such a short space of time. It is important to bear in mind that every short-term subscription converted into a long-term subscription produced a relatively large gross profit for us which, however, was not quite enough to cover the original direct mail effort. In other words, we still had a small net loss at this point.

In the following year we had a net profit which multiplied by three-fifths of our total circulation (allowing two-fifths to account for newsstand sales and a more or less permanent backlog of short-term subscriptions that would always be necessary for future growth) would give us a projected circulation profit big enough to carry the entire circulation department and pay an important part of the costs of production and distribution of the magazine, all on the basis of our experience. In the third year, our figures indicated an even bigger net profit for reasons stated below.

The above statements are not figments of my imagination nor are they the results of wishful thinking derived from hindsight. There is ample proof for them. In the four years of my administration I spent $1,200,000 (from twenty five stockholders) and not the $2,250,000 reported erroneously by

Time. This amounted to an average loss of $300,000 per annum. If I now assume that advertising, bad though it was, nevertheless paid for all its own expenses over this period as well as the expenses of the business department plus administration expense, which it did not, the only other producing department, that of circulation would have to cover all other expense, minus the net operating losses. All other expenses include the costs of the three most expensive departments: circulation, editorial and productions (printing, paper and mailing charges) averaging better than $750,000 a year, or $3,000,000 for the four year period. Deducting the $1,200,000 from the $3,000,000 mentioned above shows that Newsweek produced a gross income of $1,800,000 over the period, or an average of $450,000 a year, logically much less in the first year and much more in the fourth. Where did this money come from? There was only one place it could come from: circulation sales. In reality, income from circulation sales was paying close to two-thirds of Newsweek's total expense in the fourth year. No wonder Wilton Lloyd-Smith called Newsweek a valuable property.

Had Newsweek adopted mass methods to secure its subscriptions ,the net loss would have been at least $3,000,000 for the four-year period, probably more than $4,000,000, depending principally on the cost of obtaining each subscription. Although I am no longer familiar with current publishing economics, a fair idea of the cost of obtaining subscriptions indirectly is to compare the net profit of Time magazine with that of Newsweek. I do not know what it is, but I am confident that it will support my interpretation. Several years ago when Newsweek had approximately half Time's circulation and more than half of its advertising volume, I was informed that Newsweek's net profit was one-seventh that of time. I have no way of proving this assertion, but I am satisfied that it is close enough to the facts. Astor would have done well to have listened to me.

If any more proof is required to show that our circulation methods were intrinsically sound, it is perhaps worth repeating at this juncture for the sake of clarity and the critics just what our circulation policy was. We were editing a newsmagazine designed to appeal to intelligent people in all walks of life and we were doing it as professionals exercising our profession. We were also giving the public for the first time a choice between two newsmagazines. Everything else being equal, the law of averages would work in our favor to give us the type of reader we set out to interest. This would mean the creation of a Newsweek public from the vast pool of newsmagazine readers, not at the expense of Time, but in collaboration with it.

At the time Newsweek was started by me, Time's circulation was [   ].Today the combined circulations of Newsweek and Time is more than 5,000,000. But Newsweek could only hope to reach its sector of that great readership pool if its editorial scope and quality appealed to it. To find out in practice if it did so appeal, we had to direct our subscription canvasses to the public we wanted to reach and we thought would be interested. Pragmatically we could only do this in the beginning through the choice of mailing lists of which many are specialized, some being compiled of the names and addresses of doctors, lawyers and other professional men, others of distinctive groups of executives, such as automotive executives, etc., etc., There are many of them. Globally these were our prospects and once we had introduced some of them to Newsweek through trial offers (twenty weeks for $1) to overcome initial resistance as much as possible, the only realistic and inexpensive way we could assess their interest in Newsweek was to induce them to buy annual or two-year subscriptions for the full price.

Enough trial readers were interested enough in our newsmagazine to make the result interesting. If our cost factors had not been so high, the conversions of short-term to long-term would have given us a profit. As it was, our net conversions turned the heavy loss into a relatively small loss.

The next step was to find out how many readers who had perused Newsweek for 72 weeks would resubscribe. The results showed that for every $25,000 spent on direct mail promotion we had received back $28,500 at this point. Not as good as we had expected but with better times we could hope to improve it. When, one year later, we asked our 124-week (two years plus 20 weeks) readers to renew their subscriptions, almost all of them did, when allowances are made for changes of address, sickness, deaths and other statistical considerations. With these transactions completed our average gross profit rose to $7,700. This result was not only a highly satisfactory index of reader interest but guaranteed the profitability of our circulation methods pari passu with the consolidation of its structure by the conversions of short into long-term subscriptions. When we reached a point of equilibrium between short and long-term subscriptions, the circulation department would not only pay for itself but would contribute progressively to the cost of production and distribution of the magazine. This explains also why circulation was already paying such a large part of Newsweek's total expenses.

Once we had this type of information flowing in steadily, it was easy to determine,\ through surveys what kind of people our readers were, in the sense of occupations, incomes, ages, etc. They proved to be, as expected, the same sort of people who read Time but preferred Newsweek. It followed then logically that we had created a valuable advertising market, an important segment of the newsmagazine market. It looked on paper as though we could cash in on our experience to date. All we lacked, it appeared, was the last increase of capital, the amount of which would depend on future advertising sales.

There remains one aspect of this review to be considered: How did we go about securing the basic information concerning our conversion and renewal rates? How accurate was it? As the statistics derived there from were to constitute the means of measuring our success or failure, I kept the compilation and interpretation of them strictly in my own hands which, as publisher, I felt duty bound to do. The facts were supplied by Francis Pratt in a daily circulation report specially designed to give me the information I required. From these figures thus supplied, I could and did calculate the conversion and renewal percentage rates. Since every subscription entered on our books bore, among other information, a symbol conforming to its derivation, we knew from which lists each subscription came. By a process of elimination for unpaid short-term subscriptions, we could and did arrive at the net paid total per list. Using a modified symbol, we reached by similar means the net paid conversions to the $4 rate. And so on for renewals. It was a lot of work, and there was absolutely no chance of uncorrected error because the totals for each type of subscription must agree with the total net paid subscriptions on our books at any one time. Moreover, as already pointed out, the volume of subscription income confirms comprehensively the overall accuracy of our conversions and renewals.

To recapitulate, in four years we had built a circulation of 250,000 and of these readers, an impressive percentage of them were buying long-term subscriptions on a profitable basis to us, all on the expenditure of $1,200,000 in round figures. Who built it? I did with the devoted help and underpaid hard work of my staff. This then was the economic situation of Newsweek when I got back from my vacation in Bermuda.

When I got back to the office, a big surprise had been prepared for me by no less a person than Gene Forker, or so it seemed. Various members of my staff told me that Gene had decided he could do without me and was maneuvering to get rid of me and become the sole publisher of Newsweek. This was the last thing I had expected. Gene's duplicity was outside anything I had experienced up to that time, bearing in mind that I did not then know of Ward Cheney's tricky deceitfulness. It was utterly beyond my comprehension. His change of attitude toward me must have taken place with the connivance with one or more members of my staff, otherwise I do not think he would have dared to attempt my ouster. And undoubtedly these were the same people that Bresnahan had suborned previously. But there was no one I could point a finger to. When I was fully sure that what I had been told was true I moved against Gene, decisively. I let it be known that under no circumstances would I have anything more to do with him and forbade him entrance to our office and to further information from our records. He was later dismissed by Astor.

Meantime, what had happened to the merger? Nothing that I could find out. Wilton Lloyd Smith dodged me and I do not recall that I ever spoke to him again until he telephoned me much later on. Winky Childs knew very little more than I did, and at my request he called on Vincent Astor. He reported back the Astor appeared to be on the fence and that he did not know whether or not he would go through with the merger. Worse than this, Newsweek had been neglected for a whole month and was running up a considerable commercial debt, a state of affairs that could not be allowed to continue.

After consulting Winky, some stockholders who were still friendly to me, and some other people whose opinions I valued, I formulated a plan and got Wink to present it to his father. The plan was elastic. It allowed for the participation of Astor as well as his non-participation, and it was predicated upon the formation of a new company to take over Newsweek Inc., the acceptance of the plan by certain other designated persons, and the provision of quotas of the new capital to be reserved to the old stockholders for future subscription. Mr. Childs agreed.

There was one thing I was resolved to do, come what may: put an end to the financial nightmares that had been endemic, so to speak, since the inception of Newsweek. Perhaps it would have been wiser of me to have temporized once more, got together what immediate money I could, then have gone back to each of the old stockholders and if necessary gone after new ones. But at the time I was not prepared to undertake the risk of failure. To my mind the continuance of our financial insecurity was to jeopardize the whole future of the enterprise. Moreover, any further risk was not fair to the staff who depended for their living and their future on Newsweek,

and not fair to our readers who stood to lose part of the subscription money they had paid in good faith. It was just not
fair to anybody, including myself. It had to stop.

It was in this atmosphere that we had to calculate our financial requirements to the end of 1937. We had no time to
make extensive financial analysis and projections. We did the
best we could, relying as far as possible on our experience.
There was one imponderable in the picture: the widespread
rumor that Newsweek was in financial difficulties and was being taken over by Astor. It was even said that Today was taking over Newsweek. How much damage would this
irresponsible gossip do us? It was any man's guess. We could
only expect that it would take us many months to overcome
its effects and to allow for it in our estimates. I figured that
$500,000 would see us through, without Astor, but to be ad-
ditionally sure I doubled it. If Astor decided to come in then
the picture would be very different. We would need much
more money. How much I had no way of telling.

In order to make my plan a success, I felt I was obliged to
penalize myself, even though I did not conscientiously feel
that I was solely responsible for the current situation. Upon
the incorporation of Newsweek Inc. it was provided that I and
my key staff would have, on the basis of the capital then authorized, two-thirds of the equity. This equity was subsequently cut to one-half when the authorized capital had been
increased. Under the new plan I was to get one-third of the
equity.

After discussion with the company's council I then formed Weekly Publications Inc. with a capitalization of 300,000 no par common stock. I put a price on them of $10 a share. The original idea was to offer 200,000 shares, one half of which was to be subscribed and fully paid up, the other half to be on call or to be subscribed and paid up by Astor to the extent necessary. The remaining 100,000 shares was to be reserved for management.

When Wilton Lloyd-Smith was acquainted with the new set-up, he called me a legal thief. Strange opprobrium for a man who not long before had said I was too honest for my own good. This was over the telephone. Quite in vain that I told him I had tried to get into touch with him on several different occasions. Useless to tell him that the desperate situation of Newsweek demanded quick and resolute action. He was stone deaf to the argument that he was in no different position than anyone else, including myself. I tried to get him to come into the new deal with the others, an invitation he rejected with scorn. He was deeply offended, it seemed, because I had acted illegally behind his back, thereby contradicting himself. Apparently it was all right for him to act behind my back, but not vice versa. It developed during this strange and unexpected (by me) conversation and melancholy (for me) dialog that he had van Gerbig with him. I do not remember if Van took part in this conversation. I know he was consulted from time to time and may have been listening in. After it was over, Wilton telephoned me for an hour or more every few minutes to give vent to new vituperations. I soon decided that he and Van had been drinking too much. Whatever was left of our friendship died then and there.

A strategic move to bolster my position with those stockholders I could reach quickly and who were in a position to supply more money, was to try to interest the printer and the paper supplier. I figured that if I could interest them the stockholders would have more confidence in the new set-up, particularly in the case of McCalls who were also publishers. I succeeded with the printer but not with the paper manufacturer, who thereby lost a valuable contract. It is interesting to note that Newsweek's printing contract with McCalls has endured to the time of my writing these reminiscences in 1966. McCalls timely investment in Newsweek no doubt has been one of its most successful and remunerative.

The reason I went to see Warner, President of McCalls, was simple: Newsweek had grown mightily in importance as a client, from a few thousand copies in 1933 to some 300,000 copies a week in 1936, or better than 150,000,000 copies annually. This was a print order of no mean proportions and, I happened to know, was important to McCalls, as it paid part of the overhead of the printing plant in Dayton, Ohio. I felt that Warner could hardly help but approve of what I had done and achieved to date, and if I could persuade him to feel the same way about my proposal to recapitalize, there was a very good chance that I might get major assistance. I knew, too, that I was dealing with a very astute man, a man who knew the publishing business, who was considered a shrewd financial expert, and who was not likely to succumb to the temptation of temporary expedients. To an important extent the decision of McCalls might be decisive for me. If it were favorable, it would vindicate my judgment generally, or so I thought.

Another reason I went to McCalls was that they would recognize the necessity of quick action and would give me a decision in a matter of days, which they did. And days were all I had. I could not expect the same expedition from my old stockholders, nor did I have time to reach but a few of them. In a matter of a few days McCalls offered me $100,000 and I got $400,000 more from the old stockholders. I had still $500,000 to go.

At this point Vincent Astor decided to go ahead with the merger, no doubt aided and abetted by some of my old directors. It seemed that Astor was in complete agreement with what I had done, for he accepted it lock, stock and barrel, with only one exception: me. This was an extraordinary thing to do without ever once talking to me, and appeared to me thoroughly unscrupulous and dishonest. I do not to this day know what influenced Astor to take this step but, as I now reconstruct the scene occult forces were at work, for he asked Marvin Pierce to become provisional publisher of Newsweek, my Newsweek, until such time as he could find someone else for the job. Evidently he wanted no part of me.

Why? I felt like Huey Long must have felt just after he had been shot in the belly by an assassin. "Why?" he said to have exclaimed clutching his belly. Looking backward, I now realize that Astor killed a part of me just as surely as the assassin's bullet killed Huey Long. Why?

Actually I do not know to this day, but I can make some pretty good calculated guesses. Astor was a very rich man and had been one since birth. The loss of a few millions on Today was not a serious matter for him. Being a very rich man the Government would help him; for Astor could and doubtless would claim a tax loss. As a result of his upbringing and the power which money bought for him Astor was used to having his own way. The failure of Today would represent for him an intolerable defeat psychologically. He was not used to being thwarted. His relationship with President Roosevelt shows that. Therefore a merger with Newsweek, which was strong enough to absorb Today, provided that the only commodity that Astor had plenty of was supplied at the time of the absorption, was a welcome out for Astor. The word merger is a misnomer because Today had absolutely nothing of the least value with which to merge. But merger was the word used out of deference to Astor most probably. For Astor, Today would live in Newsweek and that would be balm enough to his ego. Therefore we may conclude that the so-called merger was a providential opportunity, an irresistible and priceless expedient with which to salve his reputation before the world.

One can imagine that Astor did not agree easily with the disappearance of Today. I suspect that one of the reasons for his delay in agreeing to the merger (let's keep on calling it that) was the inward struggle he was having over the vital question for him of whether he could manage to keep the name of Today intact. We can be sure that the absorption of Newsweek by Today was much in his thoughts. Moreover, he was strong enough, that is rich enough, to force the merger through on any terms he cared to dictate, once he had a majority of my former directors backing him up. I do not for a minute believe that it mattered one iota to Wilton Lloyd-Smith, Howell van Gerbig, or Ward Cheney whether the name Newsweek survived or not. Then why did Astor decide contrariwise? Simply because his advisors had convinced him that his only chance of success, and his advisors would have the recovery of the money lost in Today well in mind, was to let the stronger and bigger Newsweek take over. Any other course would have been suicide and Astor would have been easily convinced against another possible loss. Not only a loss of money but more importantly a loss of prestige, always close to Astor's heart. And this attitude and decision explains why Astor was willing in the years ahead to pour millions (unnecessary millions from my viewpoint) into Newsweek and accept the relatively poor results of his investment, which would be a minor point for him. What counted was success at any price.

The legality of Astor's action in grabbing Newsweek is another point in question. As it stood at the time of the merger it was unequivocally an act of piracy and not even the general release that was extorted from me alters that fact. I was the largest stockholder in both Newsweek, Inc. and Weekly Publications Inc., yet I was not consulted. Up to that time no consideration of any kind had been offered to me. It is my contention, consecrated in law and custom, that without adequate consideration in the form of reasonable compensation, the acquisition of Newsweek by Astor remains to this day illegal, and that Astor's heirs had no right whatever to dispose of Newsweek, which did not wholly belong to them, without my consent, and that therefore the sale by the Astors to the Washington Post was illegal. And these transactions will remain illegal until such time as due compensation is paid to me. It is true that when I refused to sign the general release a consideration was offered me in the form of a promise which needless to say was never kept. And as long as this promise remains unacknowledged and unredeemed, the acquisition and disposal of Newsweek remain illegal. All this will be discussed later on in the light of subsequent events.

To this day I am bothered by Astor's role in this cynical peculation. I never met the man and that I am willing to concede was as much my fault as Astor's. From what I knew of him, I was disposed to like him. Friends of mine who knew him told me that his apparent lack of intelligence, his innate desire to dominate and his aloofness were in reality due to an inferiority complex. I have no way of knowing. One judges a man by his actions in the absence of personal knowledge of him. Even so I find it difficult to associate Vincent Astor with common banditry. I knew of course, because I was told and was later to find out for myself, that he was surrounded by some unsavory characters and no doubt they had their special ways of handling him and presenting their points of view. My disinclination to think of Astor as guilty of what I shall now call euphemistically un-American behavior is supported by a letter I received from him after it was all over. The writing of that letter was not the act of an unprincipled man, but the act of a gentleman, the act of a considerate and compassionate man, not the act of atonement for a wrong committed, nor yet the cynical act of a dishonest man to appease his conscience. A robber baron would have no conscience and would have kept silent. Vincent Astor's letter rang true for no other reason than its tenor was self-evident. Nevertheless he must have felt some inner compulsion to write it.

What indeed had I done to deserve this vicious and cowardly treatment? Where had I failed? I talked with various members of my staff without finding any answer. I remember in particular talking to Bob Montgomery (?), the mercurial president of our newspaper guild, who told me in his abrupt way that everyone was upset about the merger and pronounced me as "tough but just." I thought that, especially considering its source, the finest tribute ever paid me. And of course I talked to my lawyers and I talked to Winky and probably to many other people I have forgotten about. Most of them counseled caution and patience. Something, they all thought, would be worked out for me. I had no lack of sympathizers, even to members of the staff offering to organize a strike in my favor, seriously enough to make me feel obliged to discourage it.

Marvin Pierce, tight-lipped about his appointment as provisional publisher, made it clear to me at once, as he did on many subsequent occasions, that McCall's had offered me the $100,000 and had maintained its offer after the Astor group had entered the picture. It was immaterial to McCalls who got the $100,000 so long as it served to keep Newsweek in business, because its paramount interest was to conserve the printing contract. Yet if any further proof were necessary, McCalls investment confirmed Newsweek as a valuable property just as surely as it confirmed me as responsible for it. Warner would not have recommended the investment to his board if there had been any abnormal risk involved. Normally the transfer of a creative enterprise from its creator to an alien management is fraught with risk and is usually done, when it becomes unavoidable, gradually. Why did Warner agree to run this risk? The Astor millions were undoubtedly a large part of the answer. Warner was nothing if not a realist. Of the actual discussions between McCalls and Astor I have no knowledge. My own feeling is that its willingness to invest $100,000 in Newsweek was a vote of confidence in me and that I merited some protection form Warner and Pierce. Perhaps they tried to do so. I just do not know. Judging from Pierce's attitude to me thereafter, I am inclined to think that he, at least, was not too proud of McCalls part in the pillage because he was always on the defensive with me, almost belligerently reiterating that McCalls had offered me the hundred thousand dollars in the first place No doubt that Astor's millions were the piper that called the tune.

Some attention must be paid to the Childs Family who had so faithfully and generously supported me for four years. Whatever happened, I would have to do what they wanted me to do. Old Mr. Childs was never willing to take over the financing of Newsweek but I know that he was willing to go ahead with me provided that others participated. More than that, he was willing to support me on that basis with considerably more money than his quota of the existing capital of Newsweek Inc. indicated. I could not ask for more. And I had to thank Winky for this much. I knew, too, that Mr. Childs was getting fed up with the course events were taking and that it would not have taken much to make him withdraw his support, Winky Childs notwithstanding. If I could have instantly produced $500,000 more Winky assured me that his family would go along. But that was impossible. What I lacked principally was time. With time in my favor history might have been written differently. In the end the Childs joined with the Astor group. They had to. It was the only way in which they could hope to save their considerable investment to that date. Moreover I was in favor of it on selfish grounds. With the Childs in the picture I could be sure of fair if eventual treatment.

Thus isolated I had only my duty to consider. No doubt I was a very angry man and a lot of mad thought scuttled through my brain but, after blowing off considerable steam, I had to suffocate them all. As the father of Newsweek, my first duty was to my magazine. I had to keep it alive at whatever cost to me. And for this reason alone I was not a free agent. In protecting Newsweek I was protecting my staff, most of whom had been loyal to me through very difficult circumstances. And I had to think of our readers who had supported us all magnificently. I could not let them down by any overt rebellion on my part. And I had to think of Newsweek's creditors. What indeed would happen to them if I became totally uncooperative? I could only regard them as a part of my responsibility. And lastly I had to think of the old stockholders. So far as I know, most of them preferred to lose their money rather than go in with Astor, but that does not alter the fact that at the time I felt compelled to do everything within my power to leave the way open for them to protect their individual investments in Newsweek.

Time and again I came back to the thought of why Astor was treating me as a pariah. If I had done anything, anything at all, that I could interpret as a reason for the treatment that was being handed out to me, I could have understood it. Looking backward once more I can now understand it. As I have said, Astor was used to having his own way, and as events were to confirm, he wanted his group, that is he and Averell Harriman, to be the sole owners. If it had so happened that

Astor and I had negotiated, Astor would have been in a very difficult position with me and an embarrassing one. Not only that but in a relatively weak position. In fact his only strength would have been his money. Wilton Lloyd-Smith had been quite right that we should have to save his face to get him into line. The strength of his money with me in the picture and the strength of it without me were two vastly different positions for him. However, with good will on both sides, I suppose we should have reached an agreement over who was to preside over the destinies of Newsweek.

Another vexatious problem would have been what to do with Raymond Moley. Dr. Moley had been the editor of Today and had not succeeded in attracting any following of sufficient magnitude to justify the salary of $25,000 that Astor had been paying him. More than that, I would have been against giving him or anyone else a column in Newsweek. For me, Newsweek's public is not interested in other people's opinions and interpretations, however good they may be. It would be interested in the voice of Newsweek as an experienced entity; and it had been my intention to start an editorial section in Newsweek once we had accumulated sufficient experience and were earning the money to pay for it. I surely would have had no objection to having Raymond Moley as the editor-in-chief of such a section, provided Astor had been willing to pay for it and that its policy had been politically strictly independent. There were other problems, too, that would have been very difficult of solution, such as my stock participation. Doubtless Astor had been told about these difficulties. How much easier to sidestep them by eliminating me!

Even so, I am reluctant to think of Astor as the villain of the piece. Astor had many interests and in consequence was bound to leave much of the detail of his various affairs to his subordinates. And it would be their duty, of course, to smooth out the business and legal kinks for him ahead of time, presenting him with a sort of fait accompli. In this way, he would be aware of the results and not of how they were accomplished. Astor is reported to have said at one time that there were only two advantages to being a rich man: 1) to own a yacht so that he could go anywhere he wanted and whenever he wanted; 2) to own a newspaper so that he could say what he wanted. If this be so it would argue that Astor had a peculiar interest in Newsweek. We cannot therefore lay all the blame for what happened on his side of the fence on his subordinates. Yet I do not think somehow that Astor would descend knowingly to outright robbery, no matter how legal. The sum of what I know about him leads me to the conclusion that he was a reasonable and decent man at heart, despite appearances to the contrary. And later on I had some confirmation of my opinion of him.

Somebody else had got into the act. Someone hostile to me.

Chapter Twelve

Betrayed

This trend of reasoning led me unfalteringly to one man whose subsequent behavior was to confirm him as a bad actor if not the only one. "The tree is known by its fruit." And the authority for that aphorism, as is well known, is Jesus Christ. And this particular bad man was none other than William Averell Harriman, Vincent Astor's partner on Today and his partner in the subsequent Newsweek venture. "Astor puts up the blue chips and I ante the pennies," he is reported as saying. True or not, it is certainly a statement in character with the man.

At the time Harriman entered the picture, I knew little about him, had never even met him causally and therefore had not had any kind of discussion with him. Nor was I to have any. All I did know about, that is to say almost the sum total, was what my father-in-law told me. He disliked Harriman, under whom he had worked patriotically in the Office of Price Administration, and thought of him as a spoiled rich man who picked other people's brains and used the pickings without due credit for his own purposes. Later I heard much the same thought expressed in connection with his ambassadorship in Moscow during World War II. A lot of people beside me evidently think of him as a menace to our fragile diplomacy. His egotism must have reached a pinnacle when he recently went back to Moscow for a vacation ostensibly to pass the time of day with his Communist friends but actually to try to end the Vietnam war single-handed. This must be the non plus ultra in megalomania. And again when he recently visited Brazil and other South American countries over the San Domingo intervention. The Brazilians received him politely but did not welcome his visit. Neither Harriman nor any other special ambassador was necessary. We had a perfectly good ambassador in Rio de Janeiro in the person of Lincoln Gordon who was certainly better able to present the case of the United States to the Brazilian government. And beyond this a special organization to handle Latin American affairs. Harriman's visit was just a waste of the taxpayer's money for more reason than one. All this merely indicates the man's colossal conceit. Since the pillage of Newsweek, I have heard a good many things about Harriman but rarely to his credit. Like Henry Luce, he seems to be in my small world a universally well detested man.

Harriman suddenly became very active in the so-called Newsweek merger. Once, to my knowledge, he came to the Newsweek office to see Duke, our advertising director. For some reason he had to wait and a chair was provided for him in my secretary's office, adjacent to my own. The door between the offices was open and a man I had never seen before and yet was vaguely familiar sat down. He made not the slightest move to introduce himself but sat mute and stared straight in front of himself, perhaps at me. The situation became a bit uncomfortable for me and I thought of closing the door, but I was forestalled by someone leading him off to Duke. It was only afterward that I discovered that the visitor was Harriman and it was only then that I remembered why he had seemed familiar to me: I had seen his photograph in the newspapers, possibly in Newsweek. On another occasion, later on, at the last General Motors cocktail party I attended, I was talking to Duke and one or two other people, when a man I then recognized as Harriman interrupted my conversation by saying to Duke in a loud voice "Don't forget. We are counting on you." This was before Newsweek belonged titularly to him and Astor! He got Duke all right but the marriage did not last long. Duke returned to the Time fold.

From now on a great deal of what was going on, that is that was made known to him, I got from Winky Childs, who had become Vice President of Weekly Publications Inc. Among other information I got from Winky was that Harriman did not want to have anything to do with me because, "I was too difficult to get along with." And this is from a man who is today widely known to be short tempered and difficult. One thing certain is that Harriman's opinion of me was not

his own but obtained from third parties, probably from his pal
Ward Cheney and Wilton Lloyd-Smith, his brother's pal. He
would not have received the same evaluation of my character
from anyone friendly to me, at least not in such degree, and
the inference is that he was not interested in reaching any
other conclusion. More certainly he never tried personally to
find out just how difficult I was.

How difficult is difficult? I suppose that if our basic char-
acteristics were carefully examined, most of us can be classi-
fied as difficult people. I will not deny that I am a difficult man
if by that term is meant that I have a rather turbulent temperament. I know that I am not easy to get along with. I do not
make friends readily and I have made very few of them. But
those I have made I have always kept. What Harriman doubtless meant when he said I was too difficult to get along with
was that I was too difficult to manage. If that be so than I
must agree with him, because I am not the manageable type.
I am more than willing to cooperate but I expect others to
cooperate with me. This was particularly true in Newsweek
and I had little to complain of in this respect even after the
advent of Bresnahan. That I have a very deep possessive interest in Newsweek I do not deny and perhaps I was and still
am sensitive about it. In my dealings with my staff, my directors and others I believed I had the right, and was otherwise
in a better position, to know what was best under a given set
of circumstances for the conduct of the affairs of the magazine. No doubt my directors, some of them at least, had good

reason to think of me as a difficult man. I plead guilty of brow beating them on several different occasions, in the interests of Newsweek, and no doubt they were at times thoroughly fed up with me. To an extent I sympathize with them, but not to an extent that would warrant any one of them to strike back against me with deception or vindictively to assist in my summary excommunication. After a hearing, perhaps, but even then not without some consideration. I got neither.

At this time and up to this time, I had had a considerable legal interest in Newsweek Inc. In forming Weekly Publications Inc. I had left my future participation to be decided by my performance that is measured by the results, as heretofore explained. That was a fatal error for me. What I had thought of as a square deal for the stockholders of W.P.I. proved to be a useful weapon against me in the hands of the Astor-Harriman legal sharks. No future performance, no future participation. Not legal but mighty convenient. Of course I did not know that I was to be deprived of my pecuniary interest at that time. I was soon to find out.

The day soon came when Marvin Pierce, by then my only intermediary with Astor, laid before me a document the signing of which by me, it was thought, would deprive me forever from any interest in the magazine I had originated. Not only that but I was informed by Marvin that I was to receive "severance" pay in an equal amount to that paid Gene Forker, namely $10,000. This last was just too much for me. I had created Newsweek. Without me it never would have existed.

I had a proprietary interest in it which by any decent stretch of the imagination could not be fairly taken away from me without just compensation. Yet here I was being treated as a simple employee! Up to this time, up to this very minute, I had been expecting a document to be put before me that would define my future status and interest in Newsweek. Seated at the desk from which I had conducted the affairs of Newsweek for four years, brilliantly according to some opinions, I read this document in a growing sense of dismay and re-read it in a state of shock. No status, no interest, no consideration. I was to release my interest in Newsweek for absolutely nothing in return whatever. It seemed to me that de facto it had already been done for me. All that was necessary now was the de jure finale, the last attempt to mask the robbery with a legal domino.

The merit of this accusation resides in the facts and it is perhaps worthwhile recapitulating them here even at the expense of repetition. The facts, as they related exclusively to my personal position, were that I was being asked to break off my career, surrender what reputation I had, give away the tangible results of five years of work, the not inconsiderable money I had spent in the founding of the magazine as well as the interest I had earned in compensation for the creation of it, in short a part of my very life as I then saw and felt it, and as I still see and feel it, for nothing in return, not even a minimal recognition of what I had achieved through my inventiveness, my direction and hard work. More than that, I was never to be told why I was being treated in this manner and therefore did not have any means of defending myself against the charges, if any, that were being made against me. Forgive me if I feel that the procedure used against me was and still remains antipathetic to everything the United States of America stands for and I say it as an American who, though not born in the United States, is just as patriotic as any native-born son. Any fair-minded person will agree with me, I think, even after taking into account my prejudices, that I have every reason to feel that I have been victimized and despoiled in a disgraceful and unscrupulous manner. Those are afterthoughts, but subconsciously I must have been feeling them then.

When I had recovered from the shock of reading this infamous document, I remember as clearly as if it were yesterday. I called my lawyer, told him what had happened, the gist of the contents of the general release and invited him, almost commanded him, to have dinner with me. I remember too that he did not want to come, having been absent from his hearth and home more than usually, but in the end he gave in to my insistence.

The lawyer of whom I am writing died some years ago. He was a very able lawyer and a good friend to me. For years after the events I am relating he did my legal work for me. I had complete confidence in him. He was not only sound in his knowledge of the law but had an agile and inventive Irish mind. I am withholding his name because I do not want his opinions, which were his own, to be imputed, directly or indirectly, to the law firm for which he worked for most of his lifetime, which was one of the largest and most prominent on Wall Street.

After thirty years it is no longer possible to reproduce verbatim the conversation between us which lasted some five or six hours. I remember the circumstances of it. We had dinner in a restaurant and we left to go to our respective homes at 2 o'clock in the morning, and because of this I am inclined to think that we dined and talked at Tony's. The subject of our conversation was the release of my interest in Newsweek. That much is very easy to remember. And thinking about it makes it possible for me to reconstruct it based on the subject matter, the surrounding circumstances of my own situation, questions that were uppermost in my mind, and what I remember of his responses, opinions and advice. Some of them I still remember very clearly.

My lawyer being Irish and a Catholic and enforced to suffer the prejudices against his race and religion, particularly his religion, was himself a man of prejudiced opinions, sometimes outspoken. He did not like some of the people I was up against. They were "no good". Ergo my situation was no good. In fact he had an unusually poor opinion of some of them, evidently based on what he had picked up in the "Street". And the "people" included one of my former directors.

The conversation centered on three major premises: What would happen if I refused to sign the general release and I was very disposed not to sign it; what would happen if I refused to sign it unless and until I received an adequate consideration for so doing; and in general my legal position thereafter if I were forced to sign it. All these things were discussed comprehensively.

He made it plain to me that his law firm was out of the picture and was not being consulted except by me in my capacity as a personal client. He told me that the members of the firm with knowledge of my affairs were surprised and shocked by the severity of the treatment I was receiving, but he was of the opinion that as a practical matter there was nothing I could do about it. I could fight it, of course, but he thought that that would have the same effect as refusing to sign it. He pointed out that both Astor and Harriman were very rich men and that the merger with Newsweek was not vital to their interests. He thought that if I became difficult, too difficult, they would either find some other way around my opposition or desist. Then where would I be? Where would I be with the Childs? And so on. To refuse to sign might bring a speedy and ignominious end to Newsweek. He was quite sure I did not want that. What you want is a million dollars and you can tell them all to go to hell. Perhaps this was true, but I had to have it tomorrow or the next day, and that was impossible. According to my lawyer I had no choice in the matter. I had to sign. I had to sacrifice myself for all of the people directly or indirectly interested, unfortunately including Astor and Harriman. And I had to keep in mind that the new group and its money would keep Newsweek alive. That was a major consideration for me.

When we came to an eventual monetary interest for me in payment for the work and the expense I had incurred in founding the magazine I found myself up against the same sort of argument. I just seemed to be getting nowhere. I asked him if I was supposed to give Astor and Harriman the chance to bail themselves out of their loss on Today and receive nothing for it in return. He thought I was putting the cart before the horse. No one could tell whether the chance existed in fact. Everything depended on what the new management did with Newsweek, backed by new money from Astor, Harriman, the Childs, McCalls and some of my old stockholders. He said that Astor and Harriman were putting money into the merger in the expectation of a future profit and it was that profit that would bail them out of the loss on Today. He did not seem to think it had anything to do with me. There was a lot more of this type of argument but always the same result: success would only come through new management and new money.

Then, I remember asking, I have not any claim as the originator of Newsweek to a share in the future profits of the magazine? He said I most certainly had a claim, morally and legally. Morally because whatever success the new management and the new money had would be based on what I had accomplished to date. Nobody could escape that and he thought that that position had a strong legal point to sustain it. The big point seemed to be that it would not be in my interest to press a claim at that time because the answer would be that there was nothing to pay the claim with. In other words it seemed that any claim I had or might have would be predicated firmly on Newsweek's future success. My counter argument was that they could give me stock, a percentage of Weekly Publications Inc., and that that would effectively measure the quantum of my future interest. He said they could do so but that he did not think they would and even if they did it would not guarantee me anything, for various reasons, chief of which seemed to be that they could find means and ways of eliminating my interest or reducing it to a negligible amount. And he told me how they could do it.

When I said that it appeared that I had not any legal rights whatever and that it seemed that if I were ever to obtain anything it would be dependent on Astor's and Harriman's good will, he said I had forgotten about the Childs and advised me to have a very good talk with Winky and if possible reach an understanding with him before signing the release. As to my legal rights he emphasized that it was his personal opinion and his alone that they would only become apparent in the future after success had been reached and established. He said it was on the record that I was the originator and the principal

founder of Newsweek. He said that was something that nobody could deny me including myself. He said I could do what
I liked with the rights to authorship but that he did not think
third parties would have a clear title without substantial payment to me. He said that only after success had been reached
could the quantum of substantial be defined. He thought my
position would become solid in law and equity and advised me
to ask for nothing at that time. I asked him how he could say
such things when I was being asked to waive the very rights
he said I possess. He answered that, considering all of the circumstances involved, he did not think the general release
would be worth the paper it was written on. He said that if
and when I signed the release of my interest I would be signing under duress and that would be enough to invalidate it. In
addition the absence of consideration to me personally and as
the creator of Newsweek would be decisive arguments for its
illegality.

Next morning, after a sleepless night, pondering all that
my lawyer had told, and not liking it too well, I resolved not
to sign the release unless I received a stipulated interest in
Weekly Publications Inc., and I so informed Marvin Pierce.

Then I had a long talk with Winky Childs, then the Vice
President of W.P.I. He was in a very embarrassing position
and showed it, but there was nothing he could do about it. His
father had made the decision to go ahead with Astor and that
was it. I told him about my long conversation with my lawyer
and he told me not to worry, that if and when Newsweek was

successful I would be rewarded for my services and that Astor was in agreement and that the Childs family would guarantee it. I felt better but still thought I should have it in writing. I did not say anything to Winky about that at the time, preferring to wait for Marvin Pierce's reply from Astor.

It was quite clear to me, and doubtless no less clear to Marvin Pierce, that if I refused to sign the release, McCall's printing contract would come to an end, in default of some other solution. I was pretty sure therefore that Pierce would exercise a meditorial influence in the councils of the opposition. When Marvin came with the answer, presumably Astor's, it was to repeat, almost in identical terms, what my lawyer had told me some days before. Marvin Pierce said, and I am quoting him almost verbatim, that everybody was sympathetic to my claim but that it was just not the time to ask. Newsweek was still not over the top. When it was an established success, I would be generously treated. I am not sure of the word generously; it might have been liberally or even well. I promised to think it over.

I had another conversation with my lawyer, repeated what Winky and Marvin had told me and said I thought I ought to have something in writing. He said he did not think I would get it and for reasons he had already explained he urged me not to insist. He added that so long as the Childs were in the picture he did not think I had much to worry about. If for any reason they should not be in the picture at the time Newsweek

became successful, then my position would be as he had outlined it to me. If Newsweek became successful, then my position would be as he had outlined it to me. If Newsweek never
were successful then everybody was lost. I then told him about
the $10,000 severance pay and asked him if by any stretch of
the imagination it could be construed as a consideration for
my signing the release. He said no. I asked him if he had any
changes to make in the form of the release and he said no.

Winky came to see me again and I told him about my new
discussion with my lawyer. He said he could understand why
I would want something in writing, but pointed out that it
would be almost impossible to determine a fair participation
for me. He said it would depend on how much money were
required before Newsweek went into the black and how much
of a success it was to make. I asked him why it was that Astor
was willing to promise me future fair treatment and at the
same time insist on my signing the release. He said it was Astor's legal counsel and particularly his financial man who were
insisting on the release. Astor's offer of a future consideration
was separate and he thought I could depend on it. And I could
depend on him. No, he had not talked with Averell Harriman
and anyway Harriman was a relatively minor stockholder. This
particular conversation ended I well remember with the
words, "Be a good fellow and sign it." In face of this there was
nothing else I could do.

Relying on the good faith of all concerned, I signed the release and thus ended my administrative connection with the Newsweek I had created.

At the request of the new administration I was asked to stay on in an advisory capacity. It must have been a few days after I had signed the release that I received a letter from Astor. I do not know for sure who delivered it to me but I am 99% certain it was Marvin Pierce. If it had been mailed to me, or delivered by messenger, it would have gone through my secretary's hands as she was accustomed to open all save personal mail. She does not remember the letter. Although I do not think it important it is nevertheless unfortunate that it is no longer in my possession. I think it was most probably destroyed inadvertently with a lot of other papers after Helen's death. I have found one person who, though he never saw the letter, knows of its existence. No doubt I shall find others if it becomes important. The letter said in effect that any success that Newsweek might have in the future would be built on the hard work I had done as founder and first president. This is of course self-evident but it was very nice of Astor to recognize it and write me the letter. I still appreciate it. When I showed it to Winky Childs he already knew about it and told me it had caused a sensation in the Astor headquarters and that his financial man had almost had a stroke over it, exclaiming: "Always the perfect gentleman, but spoiling everything I've done," or some such words. The first four are exact.

Why did Astor write me this letter? Because he was sorry for me? I do not think so. Because he wanted to pay a sincere tribute to me? Perhaps. Was it his way of assuring me that I should be recognized and rewarded after Newsweek had become a success? I do not know. Whatever the reason the letter still bothers me. Because of it I am unwilling to state that Astor broke his promise to me, as relayed to me by Winky Childs and Marvin Pierce. I am more inclined to think that it was overlooked, which is only an extenuation of the circumstance.

Although I was supposed to be advising the new administration, nobody asked for my advice. I do not recall one single instance when I was consulted. When I tried to give it, I had the feeling that it was no well received. And I did not get any useful information to help me. I sensed rather than knew that Today's circulation was being combined with Newsweek's on the basis that a good part of it would stick with the latter, thereby reducing or suspending for the time being our reliance on direct mail. I knew this to be a blunder of the first magnitude, and I prophesied that the million dollars put up at that time would be gone before the end of the year. I take no pride in being right.

In the first year of Astor's administration, I was told later on, more was spent than the $1,200,000 I had spent in four years. Not only had Newsweek taken on the heavy cost of transferring Today's subscriptions and also of fulfilling them. Then there was the additional burden of Moley's $25,000 and no doubt a lot of other expenses I knew nothing of including,

I suppose, a charge for Marvin Pierce's services. It was the circulation picture that disturbed me most and I warned that if our unconverted short term subscriptions were not replaced, and the timing was important, a huge deficiency would rapidly develop when Today's subscriptions started to slough off. And I said more than once that unless something effective were not done about it and at once it would cost Astor another $5,000,000 to put Newsweek over the top. I do not know, but I rather suppose that I was not far out. It would not surprise me if the blame for part at least of this huge expenditure were placed at my door. I know better.

In the spring of 1937 I took the final step and bade a sad farewell to Newsweek. My state of mind was not helped by the presentation by Kirk Sutherland, my first wife's brother, of a gold wrist watch engraved: To Tommy from his Newsweek Staff, April 1937. I still use it. Blinded by tears, Marvin Pierce saw me to the elevator, the doors opened and closed on me, separating me forever from the brain-child I had mentally sired.

Chapter Thirteen

No Justice

The immediate years following my severance were tough ones emotionally for me. My attitude was wrong but I was powerless to alter it. But time cures all things and gradually my bitterness and disappointment receded into the past and were eventually forgotten.

From time to time I saw Malcolm Muir in the Racquet Club, but he was uncommunicative. I got the impression that he had received instructions from his masters to have nothing to do with me. I did ask him to put me on Newsweek's free list so that I could follow its progress. When nothing happened I had him reminded, but still nothing happened and I desisted. Nearly 30 years later this omission, if it can be called that, was called a "silly mistake" and rectified. As I was to spend the next thirty years in South America where Newsweek is difficult to obtain, the silly mistake had the effect of anesthetizing my sensibilities as far as Newsweek was concerned.

Before that was to happen, the Childs family dropped out of the picture. Starling Childs had had enough. More than that he had lost interest. To a certain extent so had Winky. A deal was made whereby the Childs were allowed to retain 2,000 shares of Weekly Publications Inc., the remainder presumably being returned to the treasury. Mr. Childs gave 1,000 of these shares to Winky and the other 1,000 shares to me, thus honoring far beyond the call of obligation his part of the joint promise made with Astor even before Newsweek had reached the success area. It is deplorable to note in this enlightened day and age the difference in the attitude of the Childs compared with that of Astor and Harriman. The Childs who lost their entire investment of several hundred thousand dollars gave me stock that was subsequently to have a value of $50,000. Astor and Harriman who not only made a small fortune out of Newsweek but thereby recovered all of the money they lost on Today, have so far given me precisely nothing.

Except for 260 shares, I gave away and sold for a nominal price all the remaining shares that Mr. Childs gave me to the men who had helped me in founding the magazine and in the early days, including Ted Rea and Sam Williamson. Of the 260 shares I gave 100 to nominee of Mr. Childs at his request. I gave 150 shares to Helen who left them back to me when she died in 1958. The remaining 10 shares I retained for myself.

Nearly a quarter of a century later, in 1961, I first knew of Vincent Astor's death when I was notified by the Chemical Bank New York Trust Company of the sale of Newsweek by the Astor Estate to the Washington Post and of the latter's offer to buy outstanding stock of Weekly Publications Inc. at $50 per share. This news was a tremendous surprise and shock to me. I knew that Helen had been receiving dividends of $1 per share for some years but never for a moment supposed, if I ever thought of it, that it was worth anything like that figure. I promptly sold 150 shares and asked to retain 10 for old time's sake. The Washington Post did not answer my letter and it was never returned to me; but on January 8, 1962, and without reference to it I was informed that my 10 shares had been converted into "$500 principal amount of 6% debentures due December 31, 1963." The letter is noteworthy for bearing my correct address.

When the debentures were about to fall due, I was back in São Paulo and asked my son Howie to look after the redemption for me. Under the date of November 18, 1963, Howie received a letter from Frederick S. Beebe in answer to his of November 13. The last paragraph of this letter which is all that is germane to my request to be allowed to retain the aforesaid 10 shares, is quoted below:

I regret that it is not possible for us to comply with your father's wish that his 10 share ownership be preserved in the consolidation. Newsweek is very conscious of the contribution made by your father in the founding of the magazine and during the early years of its existence. Unfortunately, however, it is impossible for us to give recognition to his sentimental interest by continuing his position as a stockholder.

       Sincerely yours,

       Frederick S. Beebe

I find this a most extraordinary letter both as to content and language. In the first place it refers to a request made by me more than a year earlier without, I am reasonable certain, and solicitation on the part of my son. Why did Beebe fail to answer my letter, of which he tacitly acknowledges receipt? Instead of doing that, he informs my son of his answer, though neither requested nor authorized to do so. His obvious avoidance of putting anything in writing to me suggests that my request had been bothering him for close on to eighteen months. And note the strained language of the "contribution made by your father in the founding of the magazine." Beebe seems to be going out of his way to deny me the title of the founder of Newsweek, a title which I legally share with Edward L. Rea. Why the circumlocution? And why is it impossible to give recognition to my request? He does not owe my son that explanation, but I think he should have explained it to me. I venture to say that Beebe knows better than I do that there was nothing impossible about it. I think, too, that he had a reason for obscuring the issue.

At any rate, it was nice to know that Newsweek was "very conscious" even at that time of what I had done for it. It would be still nicer if it could find a more concrete way of expressing its consciousness.

Needless to say, the letter started me off thinking about the past and revived my memory of the promises made to me by Winky Childs and Marvin Pierce in the name of Vincent Astor. I resolved to do something about it but put action off in the expectation of visiting the States the following year. The visit did not take place because in that year I suffered a serious accident that incapacitated me for almost two years, and I did not give the matter any further thought.

Afterword

Being a first draft, there was undoubtedly more that my grandfather could have said. I do know the writing of this memoir was triggered by a letter he received in March of 1965 from John McAllister, the General Editor of Newsweek at that time. McAllister said that Newsweek was trying "to put together a definitive history of Newsweek a factual, dignified account of the birth and development of a great magazine." He wanted to "get some facts, impressions, reminiscences, and opinions from the Founding Father."

My grandfather was interested in helping what was at first stated to be published as a trade book. McAllister sent an outline of areas for discussion including my grandfather's biographical data (birthplace, boyhood education, war experience), how and when the idea for a new newsmagazine started, who were the principle backers and how they were found, his aim and formula for the magazine, who the star contributors were in the first four years, the merger with To-day, his opinion about Newsweek 's stages as well its future, anecdotes about people who made the magazine, and financial

information on the "original backing stockholding." This
struck my grandfather as being rather comprehensive and he
"had not the least objection to supplying any part of it or all
of it, provided I was to be paid reasonably and in proportion
to the work involved." He also wrote that "with the active
assistance of Newsweek we can together write a dignified and
highly interesting story and a more objective and accurate one
than I can write by myself. I am too close to and too emotionally involved in the event...to produce the desirable impartial-
ity." He felt it would take more than a year to write his part of
it. Newsweek offered him $1,000 for his time. Instead, he
wrote this memoir.

In a letter dated January 22, 1977, he wrote to me that if
his eye doctor would be able to give him new glasses so that
he could read again (he had diabetes in his later years), "I want
to write another and very important to me paper on
Newsweek. When I have done so I will send it to you." Unfortunately, I never received anything and he died in 1979.

Clearly, my grandfather's story is one-sided, although I
feel he put himself under the microscope along with the others in the story. In the words of a friend of mine, "I think
your grandfather was a remarkable man - empowered as most
great men are - by a massive ego. The founding of a successful
magazine - so successful a rival to Time - is within its own
right a significant accomplishment and a lasting monument."
I agree. He was far from a perfect man, yet his contribution
to American journalism remains.

I think he would be very proud that Newsweek has endured through several different owners and continued to lead the way in digital form, and once again in print. It would be wonderful if they put his name on the masthead as founder. In any case, his legacy continues to inform and educate intelligent readers around the world.

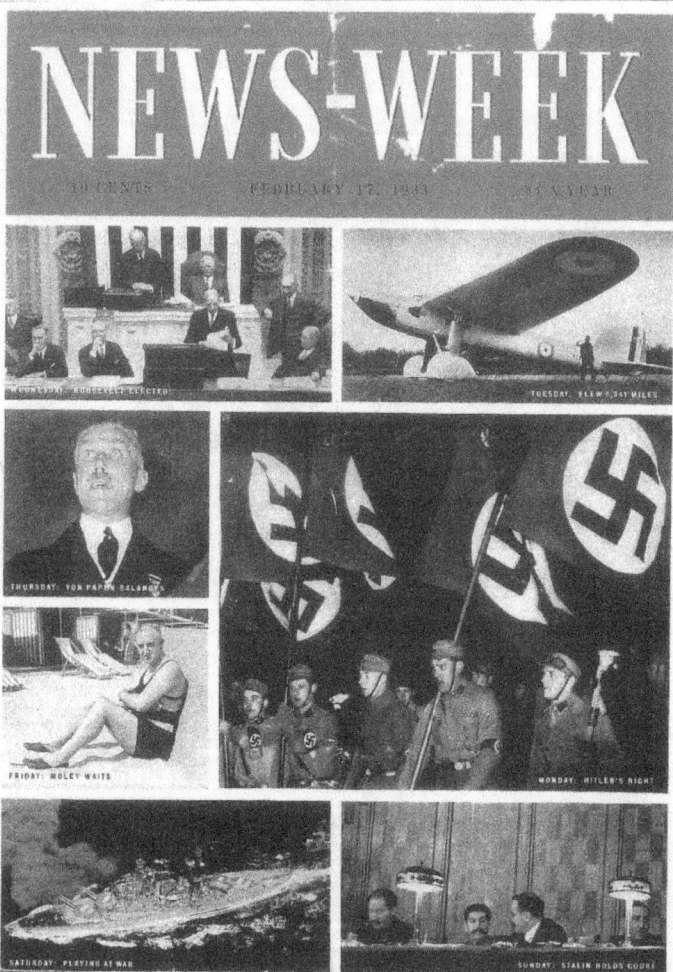

The first issue of Newsweek

NEWS - WEEK

Vol. I, No. 1   THE FRONT PAGE   Feb. 17, 1933

Easing Burdens of Debt and Foreclosure

Mortgagors, Ignoring Law, Soon Force Virtual Moratoria

Legislatures Prompt to Act

Congress Considers Measures for Early Relief of Hard Pressed Farmers, Other Home Owners

The spectre of the auctioneer stalks throughout the land, haunting debtors in city, town and country.

Next to life itself, a home is man's most prized possession. To save it, rugged individualism has grown gregarious, and harried citizens are banding against foreclosure.

Some are violent, grimly taking the law into their own hands. This was the case last week in many Mid-west States, where fulminating farmers have for two months been staging minor insurrections in farmyards, and on court house steps. Near auction blocks they hung threatening nooses, rolled foreclosure agents in the snow or forcibly rushed them from the scene. Then they held a "penny" sale, bidding in foreclosed property worth $2,000 and more for only $2 and some odd cents.

Legislatures Act

Actions of this nature resulted last week in legislative measures declaring foreclosure moratoriums in three states. In Arkansas, Governor Futrell signed a bill granting broad discretionary powers in mortgage cases to the Chancery Courts.

In Iowa, hotbed of the farm revolt because 12% of all farm mortgages are there, Governor Herring signed an act providing in effect for suspension of foreclosures until March 1, 1935.

On Tuesday the nation reeled under the news that Michigan had declared a state-wide moratorium for eight days on bank payments. As the banks closed their doors, the state securities market ceased business. In New York stock prices tumbled.

Other states throughout the Midwest farm belt are considering moratoriums. The movement seems to follow closely on the heels of the action of leading life insurance companies in proclaiming a moratorium on Iowa farm

In Deshler, Ohio: $2.17 Bid, Nothing Asked

mortgages, in response to militant activities against auctioneers' hammer.

The rising tide of necessitous mortgage relief swept down last week upon New York City, where real estate has been increasingly hard pressed. There Owen D. Young announced the formation of a comprehensive plan for refinancing mortgages, and reducing mortgage interest, with a new Realty Stabilization Corp. as its core.

The immediate aim was to provide a prop for title and mortgage companies, with nearly $5,000,000,000 of guaranteed mortgages outstanding. Of this amount, some $700,000,000 must be paid off each year. Under present conditions, many companies find this impossible.

The R. S. C. Formed

Here not individuals but corporations are asking for relief. To provide it on so large a scale, creditors have cooperated to form the Realty Stabilization Corp., subscribing $10,000,000 initially to its stock. It will make loans to the debtor companies, and where necessary, will borrow from the Reconstruction Finance Corp., which has approved its formation.

Measures of this sort, adopted and proposed throughout the nation, are merely temporary aids to debtors, pending more permanent relief. They

serve as plugs in the cracking dike of debt, weakened by depression's flood of liquidation. In past audits of economic cycles, the burden of fixed charges, hanging like a milestone around the necks of debtors, has been the last to go. Most students of the problem claim that when this weight is lifted, recovery is on the way.

Huge Sum of Private Debts

Private debts in the United States—that is, borrowing of all classes of debtors except government agencies—foot up today, roughly, to $120,000,000,000. Considerably less than half of this huge total is in the form of mortgages, now in the national spotlight.

In common parlance, a mortgage is a right to a piece of property—land or building or equipment—which the owner of the property gives as security for a loan. If he does not pay interest on the loan, or repay it at a specified time, he surrenders the property to the lender. There are different types of mortgages, some a first claim, some a second and some a third, against the property.

A foreclosure simply means that a mortgage holder forces the sale of the property because he has not been paid by the owner of the property who gave him the mortgage.

Home owners account for about

May 13 1970

Dear Annie:

Another The Weekly Newspage has come and has been,so
to speak,devoured. It is getting better,and steady improvement
is a big leaf in your crown of laurels. I know of nothing quite
like it,and have never known anything like it. It is original,
informative and entertaining. Keep it that way.

Starting a publication,any well-intentioned publication,is an act of friendship. You make friends with a lot
of people,many of whom you will never know. And they will not
only make friends,(sometimes critical friends) with you,but they
will begin to rely on you as well as support you. The fundamental
difference between you and them is that all of your public will
get to know you.

So,whether you like it or not,your reputation Becomes
involved,if not at stake.

You are with every new issue contributing to a chapter in the annals of American Journalism. You are entitled to be
proud of yourself. Have you ever thought of it that way?
       Much love,
         Gpa

PS. Mary failed to get the parcel off in Santos,but we will try
again in Itajai. One way or another we will get it off - eventually.

Letter from Thomas J. C. Martyn to his granddaughter (see page 9)

Oil portrait of Captain Thomas J. C. Martyn that hung in his son's family dining room.

Thomas J. C. Martyn

Thomas J. C. Martyn & Anne Martyn Alexander, Brazil, 1975

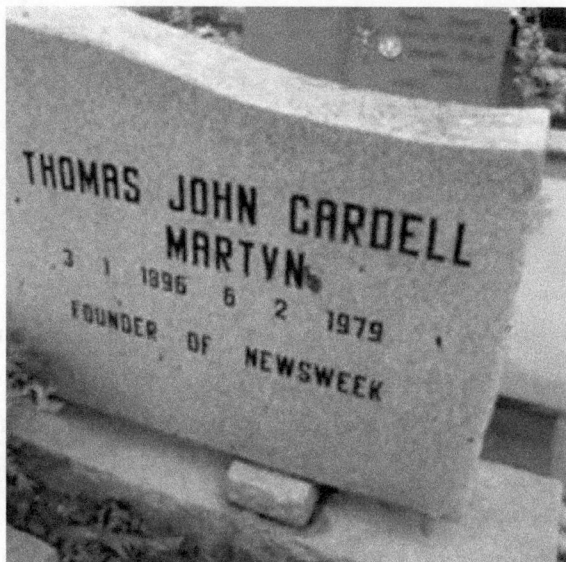

Gravestone in Agrolandia, Brazil

Acknowledgments

My father, Howell Cheney Martyn, didn't know what to do with his father's manuscript, but he held onto it, for which I am very grateful. My mother, Celia G. Martyn, encouraged and financed the trip to Brazil to see my grandfather in the summer of 1975, the last time I saw him. She also told me stories about my grandfather, helping fill in the blanks. Thanks to my sister and brother, Amy E. Martyn and Thomas H. Martyn, for their enthusiastic support. Nancy Purcell and Michael Trufant gave vital guidance along the way, for which I am grateful. Thanks also to Krista Lunsford, Stacey Lunsford, Andrea Stolz, Jerry Schwartz, Harry Gilliam, Gail Zawacki, Harry Gibbs, Joseph Cincotta, David Fleming, Debra Lieb, Nancy Mason, Don Sinclair, Pat Childress, Bill Roseen, Brenda Wiley and Carol Clay. As always, author Susan Gabriel provided invaluable support, insight and editorial expertise. Numerous other individuals supported this project: I am grateful for all of you.

— Anne Martyn Alexander

About the Authors

Thomas J.C. Martyn (1896–1979) was the founder of *Newsweek*, the second-largest news magazine in the history of the United States. The son of a British soldier, Martyn served as a pilot in World War I, losing a leg in an aviation accident. His World War One experience is chronicalled in *Aviation Adventures: The True Story of the World War 1 Royal Flying Corps Pilot Who Founded Newsweek*. After the war he was recruited as *Time*'s first foreign editor. He served there under the founder, Briton Hadden, then worked for the *New York Times* before raising capital to start *Newsweek*. He published the first edition in 1933, at the height of the Great Depression. After years of financial struggle and internecine conflict, Martyn was ousted from the board. A few years later, he went to South America to pursue a new business venture, and spent the remaining years of his life there.

www.InsideTheFoundingOfNewsweek.com

Anne Martyn Alexander, the granddaughter of Thomas J.C. Martyn, runs a coaching company specializing in business development, working with entrepreneurs throughout the U.S. and Europe. For over 25 years she has worked in and advised businesses, with experience in construction, commercial real estate, food manufacturing, engineering, and business brokerage. More information at Authentic-Alternatives.com.

Aviation Adventures

The True Story of the World War 1
Royal Flying Corps Pilot Who Founded Newsweek

By
Thomas J. C. Martyn

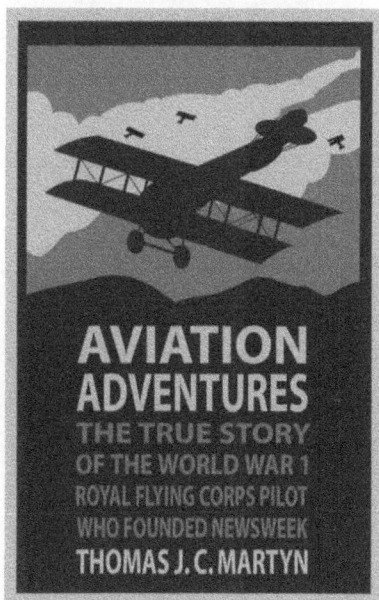

On February 17, 1933, Newsweek magazine published its very first issue. Thomas J.C. Martyn had envisioned a national weekly news magazine for a decade and had worked to accomplish that goal with the tireless zeal and dedication of a true entrepreneur. What kind of man has the vision, creativity and dedication to accomplish such a big dream? *Aviation Adventures* contains some answers to that question.

Nineteen years earlier, when World War One broke out in 1914, Martyn was a bright eyed 18 year old, full of romantic and patriotic ideas. He joined the British Royal Air Corps, an elite fighting organization that garnered the respect of an entire nation. The air battles he participated in, the respect he earned from his commanding officers and fellow pilots and his behind-the-scenes contributions reveal the character of the man and journalist who would go on to found Newsweek.

Aviation Adventures: The True Story of the World War 1 Royal Air Corps Pilot Who Founded Newsweek is Martyn's personal account of how he was able to wrangle a much coveted acceptance into the Royal Flying Corps. It then details the bombing raids and other contributions he made to the war effort.

Written in the detailed and colorful language of the journalist Martyn was to become, *Aviation Adventures* provides an up close and personal look at one man's World War One wartime experience.

The first chapter follows.

For King and Country

When Sir Edward Grey's ultimatum to the Government of Kaiser Wilhelm II of Germany expired on August 4, 1914, not only did the lights start to go out one by one all over Europe but the sun began to set on what had been revered as the impregnable British Empire. Had I known this at the time as one of the consequences of the war, my patriotic fever might have been cooled. To a romantically inclined lad of eighteen, the war appealed to me as a great adventure, and my one thought was to get me to England without delay to offer my sword, as soon as I could get one, to my King and Country.

When what was to become World War I began, I was in Penticton, a Canadian Pacific Railway summer resort at the southern tip of the Okanagan Lake in British Columbia, Canada. My instant reaction was to join my regiment in England. Actually, I had no regiment and even if I had one I was thousands of miles away from it. What I knew in my innermost mind was that I would have, as the son of a British army officer, little difficulty in securing one. I tried to pedal that without the least success. I asked the Canadian Pacific Railway to give me a pass to England. These people were my friends and I hoped, indeed I expected, them to concede me a pass without question. That they would not do. They were willing to give me a pass as far as Quebec, provided I could prove that a commission awaited me in England. This I could not do. The CPR attitude appeared to me as so much red tape. I did not consider the responsibilities involved.

Having pursued the possibilities of getting myself transportation free to England to a dead end, I began to canvass alternatives. I figured that once in London I had sufficient cash to keep afloat until I could get my application for a commission processed. The problem was getting myself from Penticton there. I thought briefly of seeking help from my stepfather but for some reason or other thought the better of it. A grave error as it turned out. The only way out was to take the advice of my friends and enlist in the Canadian Army, and apply for a commission when I got to England. And that is precisely what I did.

All this indecision was taking too much time and the war was nearly over now and probably would be over long before I got to England. These were my anxious thoughts as I left Penticton for Vancouver, even farther away from England, and thence to Victoria, still farther away. I would say that the war was some three months old before I began my active training with the Canadian Army. I did not enjoy. I was much too impatient to be off for England. My patriotism was not that of the common man but of the chevalier sans peur variety. Only in that way could I hope to achieve glory and a baton of a field marshal.

Even as common soldier, my superior military genius was at once apparent; I was promoted in the (training) field to corporal, skipping the intermediate rank of lance corporal. In reality this promotion was more due to nepotism than to merit. I was fortunate to know several families living in Victoria, and it so happened that I was in a platoon commanded by the son of one of them.

Our training was perfunctory and consisted in producing physical fitness through plenty of drilling and route marching. Every effort was made to get us ready for the long journey to England in record time. We were a mixed crew. All of us were volunteers and came from diversified strata in the social order. Some were rich men and boys. Some were university graduates. Most of them came from commerce and from farms in the interior. Socially there was little or no difference between us and our officers. Looking back, it was criminal folly to expend such men as mere cannon fodder, which was later done with most of them.

THE DAY finally came in the spring of 1915 when we took leave of Victoria for the wearisome journey to the port of Rimouski on the St. Lawrence River. A large crowd of people came to see us off, among them hundreds of girls bearing gifts and shedding tears. The journey to Rimouski passed without event in the utmost boredom. At Rimouski we were stowed away aboard a transport ship like so much cargo. The extreme discomfort of our living conditions lasted some ten days before we disembarked at Liverpool. The tedious voyage across the North Atlantic was relatively unexciting. We and some other transport and cargo ships were heavily escorted by destroyers of the Royal Navy and the Royal Canadian Navy. We had a number of scares related to the presence and activities of German submarines, but we heard and saw nothing of them. Only the fact that we were alerted several times testified to the presence of a lurking danger.

Upon our arrival in England we were sent to Aldershot where the regiment was quartered until it was sent as a unit to France. What I remember most vividly was the sight of field marshal Lord Kitchener on his white horse, surrounded by a large entourage of military aids, the Union Jack fluttering overhead, who had come to inspect us. It was a truly magnificent and awe inspiring sight. This must have been very shortly before he went to his doom in the Baltic Sea.

In accordance with information I received much later on, hardly any of the officers and men of the Canadian regiments survived that winter in Flanders.

It had been my intention to use my family connections to help me get a commission in the British Army, but fortuitously the initiative was directed through another channel. By this time it had become generally known that the British Army was desperately short of officers and was looking for replacements in every nook and cranny offering a possibility. Hence the invitation to the Canadian forces.

With the utmost dispatch I filled in an application form which my then commanding officer approved and some thirty days later was commissioned a Second Lieutenant in the Third Battalion (London Regiment) Royal Fusiliers.

The month I spent waiting for my commission was covered by sick and ordinary leave. First I contracted a mild dose of jaundice and became as yellow as an indigenous peasant of the Yellow Race. I suffered little inconvenience other than being promptly nicknamed Chink. Second, I had a slight accident. Bicycling away from camp at high speed along a lane leading to the main road, I put the brakes on a bit too fast. The bicycle skidded in a pocket of sand and I was thrown violently some six or eight fee into a prickly hedge. My uniform was ruined and I was pretty well scratched up. The bicycle was undamaged.

My ordinary leave was spent on my honeymoon following my marriage to Sheila Sutherland who had followed me from Canada, braving the dangers of the North Atlantic. It wasn't a very good time in which to get married, with rationing and whatnot, but we made the most of it.

Soon after our wedding, notice of my commission appeared in the Royal Gazette. After spending some ten days getting me outfitted we reported to the regiment at Beckenham, a village on the outskirts of London. We had the good fortune to be billeted with a very nice couple who "did" for us more as if we were their son and daughter than as paying guests.

It appeared that I was the only new officer to report at Beckenham. I was particularly irked to be ordered to present myself soon after dawn every morning except Sunday for "physical jerks", I, an officer, and full of my dignity as such, with the rank and file under the regimental Sergeant Major. To make it worse, I was the only commissioned officer forced to undergo the humility, as I thought of it, of having of having to obey a noncommissioned officer, a situation in which he took particular delight, a differential delight albeit with a "No then, sir, a little quicker, if you please." Always respect for my rank, even to the grinning salute off the barrack square when he chanced to meet me. Later on I was to have a profound respect for this man who became of solid assistance to me.

Our colonel and commanding officer had been recalled from retirement. He was upward of sixty years of age, a handsome, soldierly figure of a man, with a ruddy complexion and the whitest of mustaches. He had served long and meritoriously in the Indian Army, judging from his rows of ribbons. He was a stickler for army etiquette and a strict disciplinarian. He was charming to Sheila, but that did not get me the slightest favor from him. For instance, I was obliged to attend the regular Thursday night mess dinner, come what may.

We did not stay long at Beckenham and were moved to Salisbury Plains where, little did we know it, we were to become a training center for new recruits and later for Derby draftees. Sheila came along too and we were billeted in a tiny house in a nearby village.

The new recruits were a motley group of men mostly from the East end of London. A few of them, the best of them, were very fine men indeed who took their military life seriously and subsequently made good if several noncommissioned officers. Most of them were a bunch of undisciplined hooligans, very difficult to handle and train. From thereon they tapered off to what today would be called retarded mentalities. Some were so hopeless that they had to be returned to civilian life. It was impossible to imagine why such individuals were not screened before they reached the induction stage. But once in the army it was enormously difficult to get them out.

Once the sergeant of my platoon came to me in despair. He had been trying to get one of these misfits, in all other respects a beguiling and eager youngster, to salute alternately with his left and then his right hand. In the British army, a private salutes with the hand farthest away from the officer he is passing. I took a turn trying to teach this boy the difference between his right and left hand. It was hopeless. Had it not been for his cheerfulness, his ever ready and patient desire to please, and his enormous pride in being a soldier, he would not have lasted ten minutes.

Sometime later on when I was acting as Officer of the Day, one of my duties was to preside over the ceremony of hoisting the Union Jack at sunrise and lowering it at sundown.

On one particular day, and a very wet day it was, I chanced to pass this young recruit on my way to the sundown rites. The mud was inches thick underfoot. He had been sent to the camp post office to collect the mail for his platoon and his arms were full of letters, newspapers, magazines and parcels, so full that I could barely see his face. Suddenly he caught sight of me and in a flash came up with a double handed salute letting his precious burden fall into the mire. I do not remember what happened to him after that.

Our life on Salisbury Plains was spend in drilling these men on the parade ground and taking them on progressively longer route marches (pronounced raut marches). The earlier marches were nothing short of pathetic. These city bred boys had never walked so far in months the distances they were now required to cover in a matter of hours. The anguish was apparent. Many a time I carried the pack and rifle of some poor devil who could hardly drag one foot in front of the other. When we came back to camp, it was the custom to march at attention while the band broke out into the martial music of the regimental march. It was then easy to spot the difference between the regular or well-trained soldier and the recruit. The latter were too far done to give a damn, despite the exhortations of their non-commissioned officers, while the former snapped to attention and marched with ramrod precision. But as the recruits became hardened, they too became imbued with the regimental esprit de corps and marched like veterans. It was impossible not to feel proud of them. It was impossible not to feel proud of them. It was the visible result of our personal success with them. And it was our only reward, a satisfying reward.

Up to around this time, the British Army was being trained in accordance with a manual established perhaps fifty years before. It consisted, besides physical fitness drills, of little more than bayonet fighting and rifle practice, at least insofar as the infantry was concerned. By this time the fighting in France and Flanders had bogged down into trench warfare, which was bringing into existence new weapons. There was not an officer among us who knew anything about them. Thus we were unable for a while to teach our men the use, care and maintenance of the Lewis machine gun. We did not have one and even if we had had one, there was nobody around who knew how to operate it. And so it was with hand grenades, poison gases, trench construction and tactics. Besides this, there were no facilities for teaching and training.

The War Office was fully aware of these deficiencies and quickly set up specialized schools in each Command, using for the most part survivors from Mons and Ypres. These veterans were of course numerically limited insofar as availability was concerned and could by no stretch of the imagination be used to instruct the large number of units comprising the New Army in formation. The plan was to use these specialized schools to teach officer instructors who would return to their regiments to set up battalion schools for the training of permanent instructors, who would in turn train officers and men.

The sheer weight of numbers was against any other method. After the Derby recruits (draftees) made their appearance, our regiment swelled to some 3,000 officers and men. I was commanding a platoon the size of a battalion, or close to it.

The state of affairs was to alter radically my military career. In the space of a few months, I was sent to five different schools and became "expert" on the Lewis machine gun; the composition, construction and employment of various types of hand grenades; the construction of trenches and the tactical use of them; the use of various types of poison gas and gas masks; and, finally, I was sent to a staff course at the General Staff college at Camberwell. After each of the first four courses, I returned to my regiment with considerable equipment, set up a training center, and as soon as it began to function well, I was sent off to a new course.

On my return from the grenade school, I was allotted a section of a hut in which to demonstrate my wares. I set out on a table various specimens of grenades, some sectional to show their inner mechanisms, some live, in separate groups. There were a number of diagrams and charts to be hung. Instructing the sergeant I had selected, or who had been selected for me, where to hang them I went off to attend to something else. I had not got far when I was brought short by a loud explosion. Rushing back to the Grenade School hut, I found the place in a shambles and the sergeant, white as a sheet, in a dazed condition. The silly fellow had used a stick grenade to hammer a nail into the wall for one of the charts and it had exploded in his hand. It was a miracle that he was uninjured.

My involvement in this training program, useful and interesting though it was, became increasingly distasteful to me. I had volunteered for King and Country, for a War to end Wars, for Freedom and Democracy and whatever slogans were rife at the time. More than anything, I had volunteered to fight and fight was what I was determined to do. But every time I applied to be sent to the regiment in France, I was rewarded by being sent on another course, always with some explanation that the service I was performing was more valuable to King and Country than fighting overseas.